Hymns for the Revised Common Lectionary

2007

Hymns for the Revised Common Lectionary

2007

Dean B. McIntyre

DISCIPLESHIP RESOURCES

P O BOX 340003 • NASHVILLE, TN 37203-0003
www.discipleshipresources.org

ISBN 13: 978-0-88177-489-4
ISBN 10: 0-88177-489-8
Library of Congress Control Number 2006932559

DR 489

Introduction

This volume contains lists of congregational hymns and songs for use with readings from *The Revised Common Lectionary* for calendar year 2007.
Recommended titles are provided for every Old Testament, Psalm, Epistle, and New Testament reading for every Sunday and major observance of the liturgical year. It is intended to supplement but not replace the Index of Topics and Categories (Topical Index) found in the back of most hymnals.

Although worship planners of many denominations will find this volume useful, it is particularly designed for use by United Methodists. Every hymn title is listed with its number in the major hymnals and songbooks of the denomination:

UMH   *The United Methodist Hymnal* (Nashville: The United Methodist Publishing House, 1989)

MVPC   *Mil Voces Para Celebrar: Himnario Metodista* (Nashville: The United Methodist Publishing House, 1996)

CLUW   *Come, Let Us Worship: The Korean-English United Methodist Hymnal; Book of United Methodist Worship* (Nashville: The United Methodist Publishing House, 2001)

TFWS   *The Faith We Sing* (Nashville: Abingdon Press, 2000)

SOZ   *Songs of Zion* (Nashville: Abingdon Press, 1981)

These titles may easily be cross-referenced with the contents of other hymnals and songbooks. Some hymns and songs are listed twice because they are frequently known and identified by two titles, such as "Hymn of Promise" and "In the Bulb There Is a Promise." Some others are listed twice if they appear in two languages, such as "Cuando El Pobre" and "When the Poor Ones."

Dean B. McIntyre
Director of Music Resources
The Center for Worship Resourcing
The General Board of Discipleship of The United Methodist Church
P.O. Box 340003
Nashville, TN 37203-0003
Telephone 615-340-7073

January 1, 2007 (New Year's Day)

Scripture Hymn Title	UMH	MVPC	CLUW	TFWS	SOZ
Ecclesiastes 3:1-13					
For the Fruits of This Creation	97				
O God, Our Help in Ages Past	117				
Great Is Thy Faithfulness	140	30	81		
All Things Bright and Beautiful	147		63		
Forth in Thy Name, O Lord, I Go	438				
By Gracious Powers So Wonderfully Sheltered	517				
Beams of Heaven as I Go	524				10, 207
God of the Ages	698	377			
Hymn of Promise	707	338	392		
In the Bulb There Is a Flower	707	338	392		
From the Rising of the Sun				2024	
I Was There to Hear Your Borning Cry				2051	
For One Great Peace				2185	
In His Time				2203	
Psalm 8					
All Creatures of Our God and King	62	22			
Praise, My Soul, the King of Heaven	66				
O Lord My God! When I in Awesome Wonder	77	2	61		
How Great Thou Art	77	2	61		
Joyful, Joyful, We Adore Thee	89	5	75		
For the Beauty of the Earth	92	8			
For the Fruits of This Creation	97				
God, Whose Love Is Reigning o'er Us	100		73		
O God, Our Help in Ages Past	117				
O God in Heaven, Grant to Thy Children	119		227		
Children of the Heavenly Father	141		335		

7

Scripture Hymn Title	UMH	MVPC	CLUW	TFWS	SOZ
Many and Great, O God, Are Thy Things	148	50	71		
God Created Heaven and Earth	151				
I Sing the Almighty Power of God	152		65		
Creator of the Earth and Skies	450				
Prayer Is the Soul's Sincere Desire	492				
O God Beyond All Praising				2009	
Great Is the Lord				2022	
How Majestic Is Your Name				2023	
From the Rising of the Sun				2024	
Awesome God				2040	
Amen, We Praise Your Name, O God				2067	
Glory to God in the Highest				2276	

Revelation 21:1-6a

Scripture Hymn Title	UMH	MVPC	CLUW	TFWS	SOZ
O God, Our Help in Ages Past	117				
There's Something About That Name	171	74			
There's a Spirit in the Air	192				
O Let the Son of God Enfold You	347	190	91		
Spirit Song	347	190	91		
This Is a Day of New Beginnings	383	208	311		
Love Divine, All Loves Excelling	384				
O Come and Dwell in Me	388				
For the Healing of the Nations	428				
My Faith Looks Up to Thee	452				215
Come, Ye Disconsolate, Where'er Ye Languish	510				
Beams of Heaven as I Go	524				10, 207
We Shall Overcome	533		140		127
Here, O My Lord, I See Thee	623				
This Is the Feast of Victory	638				
Sing with All the Saints in Glory	702		382		
Soon and Very Soon	706		385		198
Come, Let Us Join Our Friends Above	709		387		
I Want to Be Ready	722				151
O Holy City, Seen of John	726		390		
O What Their Joy and Their Glory Must Be	727				
From the Rising of the Sun				2024	

Scripture Hymn Title	UMH	MVPC	CLUW	TFWS	SOZ
Awesome God				2040	
Open Our Eyes				2086	
We Will Glorify the King of Kings				2087	
All Who Hunger				2126	
You Who Are Thirsty				2132	
Blessed Quietness				2142	
O Freedom				2194	
Joy Comes with the Dawn				2210	
I'll Fly Away				2282	
For All the Saints				2283	
Joy in the Morning				2284	

Matthew 25:31-46

Scripture Hymn Title	UMH	MVPC	CLUW	TFWS	SOZ
How Can We Name a Love	111				
O God, Our Help in Ages Past	117				
We Gather Together to Ask the Lord's Blessing	131	361			
Christ Is the World's Light	188				
There's a Spirit in the Air	192				
Jesus' Hands Were Kind Hands	273		176		
Crown Him with Many Crowns	327	157			
Where Cross the Crowded Ways of Life	427	296			
For the Healing of the Nations	428				
Jesu, Jesu, Fill Us with Your Love	432	288	179		
All Who Love and Serve Your City	433				
Cuando El Pobre Nada Tiene	434	301	138		
When the Poor Ones Who Have Nothing	434	301	138		
Come, Ye Disconsolate, Where'er Ye Languish	510				
Forward Through the Ages	555				
Lord, Whose Love Through Humble Service	581				
Rescue the Perishing	591				
When the Church of Jesus Shuts Its Outer Door	592				
Come, Sinners, to the Gospel Feast (Communion)	616				
I Come with Joy to Meet My Lord	617				
Come, Ye Thankful People, Come	694		241		

Scripture	Hymn Title	UMH	MVPC	CLUW	TFWS	SOZ
	God Weeps				2048	
	Shout to the Lord				2074	
	Carol of the Epiphany				2094	
	Star-Child				2095	
	All Who Hunger				2126	
	Sunday's Palms Are Wednesday's Ashes				2138	
	What Does the Lord Require of You				2174	
	Together We Serve				2175	
	Wounded World that Cries for Healing				2177	
	Here Am I				2178	
	For One Great Peace				2185	
	Now It Is Evening				2187	
	People Need the Lord				2244	
	In Remembrance of Me				2254	
	As We Gather at Your Table				2268	
	Come, Share the Lord				2269	

January 6, 2007 – Epiphany of the Lord

(Note: Epiphany may be observed on Sunday, December 31, 2006 using these readings.)

Scripture Hymn Title	UMH	MVPC	CLUW	TFWS	SOZ
Isaiah 60:1-6					
Immortal, Invisible, God Only Wise	103		74		
Rise, Shine, You People	187				
Break Forth, O Beauteous Heavenly Light	223				
From a Distant Home	243				
De Tierra Lejana Venimos	243				
O Morning Star, How Fair and Bright	247				
We've a Story to Tell to the Nations	569				
Rise Up, O Men of God	576				
This Little Light of Mine	585		338		132
O Splendor of God's Glory Bright	679				
Arise, Shine Out, Your Light Has Come	725				
Arise, Shine				2005	
Honor and Praise				2018	
Glory to God				2033	
We Are Called				2172	
Shine, Jesus, Shine				2173	
Light of the World				2204	
Gather Us In				2236	
Psalm 72:1-7, 10-14					
Now Thank We All Our God	102				
Jesus Shall Reign Where'er the Sun	157				
Come, Christians, Join to Sing	158				
At the Name of Jesus Every Knee Shall Bow	168				
Word of God, Come Down on Earth	182				
My Soul Gives Glory to My God	198				
Tell Out My Soul, the Greatness of the Lord	200				

Scripture	Hymn Title	UMH	MVPC	CLUW	TFWS	SOZ
	Hail to the Lord's Anointed	203	83			
	The Gift of Love	408		341		
	Though I May Speak with Bravest Fire	408		341		
Ephesians 3:1-12						
	Ye Servants of God, Your Master Proclaim		181			
	Christ Is the World's Light	188				
	Go, Tell It on the Mountain	251	97			75
	Prayer: Epiphany	255				
	We Would See Jesus	256		168		
	Blessed Assurance	369	65	287		
	Make Me a Captive, Lord	421				
	Christ, from Whom All Blessings Flow	550		250		
	Christ Is Made the Sure Foundation	559				
	Grace Alone				2162	
	We Are Called				2172	
	Song of Hope				2186	
	We Are God's People				2220	
Matthew 2:1-12						
	Alleluia	186		355		
	Lo, How a Rose E'er Blooming	216				
	What Child Is This	219	112	154		
	Angels from the Realms of Glory	220				
	In the Bleak Midwinter	221				
	Niño Lindo, Ante Ti Me Rindo	222	114			
	Child So Lovely, Here I Kneel Before You	222	114			
	O Little Town of Bethlehem	230	94			
	Sing We Now of Christmas	237		166		
	Angels We Have Heard on High	238	98			
	De Tierra Lejana Venimos	243				
	From a Distant Home	243				
	'Twas in the Moon of Wintertime	244				
	The First Noel	245	89			
	O Morning Star, How Fair and Bright	247				
	On This Day Earth Shall Ring	248				
	There's a Song in the Air	249				
	Go, Tell It on the Mountain	251	97			75

Scripture	Hymn Title	UMH	MVPC	CLUW	TFWS	SOZ
	We Three Kings	254	108			
	Epiphany *(Prayer)*	255				
	We Would See Jesus	256		168		
	Now the Silence	619				
	Honor and Praise				2018	
	Give Thanks				2036	
	Jesus Be Praised				2079	
	Carol of the Epiphany				2094	
	Star-Child				2095	
	Rise Up, Shepherd, and Follow				2096	
	The Virgin Mary Had a Baby Boy				2098	

January 7, 2007 (Baptism of the Lord/ First Sunday after Epiphany)

Scripture Hymn Title	UMH	MVPC	CLUW	TFWS	SOZ
Isaiah 43:1-7					
Canticle of the Holy Trinity	80				
We Believe in One True God	85				
The God of Abraham Praise	116	28			
Lonely the Boat, Sailing at Sea	476				
Thy Holy Wings, O Savior	502				
Stand By Me	512				41
When the Storms of Life Are Raging	512				41
How Firm a Foundation	529	256			
The Church's One Foundation	545	269	255		
The Church's One Foundation	546				
In Christ There Is No East or West	548				65
Lord God, Almighty				2006	
Eternal Father, Strong to Save				2191	
You Are Mine				2218	
Psalm 29					
Holy, Holy, Holy! Lord God Almighty	64	4	79		
¡Santo! ¡Santo! ¡Santo!	65	4			
Gloria, Gloria in Excelsis Deo! *(canon)*	72		353		
O Worship the King, All-Glorious Above	73				
Source and Sovereign, Rock and Cloud	113				
God of the Sparrow God of the Whale	122	37	59		
Praise to the Lord, the Almighty	139	29	68		
Many and Great, O God, Are Thy Things	148	50	71		
I Sing the Almighty Power of God	152		65		
Praise and Thanksgiving Be to God	604		230		
Let All Things Now Living				2008	

Scripture Hymn Title	UMH	MVPC	CLUW	TFWS	SOZ
We Sing of Your Glory				2011	
Holy				2019	
Great Is the Lord				2022	
Glory to God				2033	
Blessed Be the Name of the Lord				2034	
Father, I Adore You				2038	
Awesome God				2040	
Shout to the Lord				2074	
You Alone Are Holy				2077	
Holy, Holy, Holy Lord				2256	

Acts 8:14-17

Jesus! the Name High over All	193		199		
We Meet You, O Christ	257				
Breathe on Me, Breath of God	420				
Filled with the Spirit's Power	537				
O Spirit of the Living God	539				
See How Great a Flame Aspires	541		248		
Like the Murmur of the Dove's Song	544				
This Is the Spirit's Entry Now	608				
Holy Spirit, Come to Us				2118	
Come, Holy Spirit				2125	
Wonder of Wonders				2247	
Baptized in Water				2248	
God Claims You				2249	
I've Just Come from the Fountain				2250	
We Were Baptized in Christ Jesus				2251	
Come, Be Baptized				2252	

Luke 3:15-17, 21-22

At the Name of Jesus Every Knee Shall Bow	168				
Jesus! the Name High over All	193		199		
Blessed Be the God of Israel	209				
When Jesus Came to Jordan	252	125			
Prayer: Baptism of the Lord	253				
We Meet You, O Christ	257				
Spirit of Faith, Come Down	332		219		
Spirit Song	347	190	91		

Scripture	Hymn Title	UMH	MVPC	CLUW	TFWS	SOZ
	Breathe on Me, Breath of God	420				
	Like the Murmur of the Dove's Song	544				
	Praise and Thanksgiving Be to God	604		230		
	Wash, O God, Our Sons and Daughters	605				
	Come, Let Us Use the Grace Divine	606				
	This Is the Spirit's Entry Now	608				
	We Know That Christ Is Raised	610		231		
	Child of Blessing, Child of Promise	611		232		
	God the Sculptor of the Mountains				2060	
	Jesus, Name above All Names				2071	
	Wild and Lone the Prophet's Voice				2089	
	Spirit of God				2117	
	She Comes Sailing on the Wind				2122	
	Shine, Jesus, Shine				2173	
	Wonder of Wonders				2247	
	Baptized in Water				2248	
	God Claims You				2249	
	I've Just Come from the Fountain				2250	
	We Were Baptized in Christ Jesus				2251	
	Come, Be Baptized				2252	
	Water, River, Spirit, Grace				2253	

January 14, 2007 (Second Sunday after Epiphany)

Scripture Hymn Title	UMH	MVPC	CLUW	TFWS	SOZ
Isaiah 62:1-5					
We, Thy People, Praise Thee	67		72		
Holy God, We Praise Thy Name	79		80		
Joyful, Joyful, We Adore Thee	89	5	75		
God of Many Names	105				
Lift Every Voice and Sing	519				32
Are Ye Able, Said the Master	530	300			
We've a Story to Tell to the Nations	569				
As Man and Woman We Were Made	642				
I Know Not Why God's Wondrous Grace	714		290		
I Know Whom I Have Believed	714		290		
Battle Hymn of the Republic	717				24, 213
Mine Eyes Have Seen the Glory	717				
My Lord, What a Morning	719		386		145
Psalm 36:5-10					
God of Many Names	105				
How Can We Name a Love	111				
How Like a Gentle Spirit	115		216		
Great Is Thy Faithfulness	140	30	81		
On Eagle's Wings	143		83		
O Love, How Deep, How Broad, How High	267				
Love Divine, All Loves Excelling	384				
Come, Thou Fount of Every Blessing	400	42	127		
Thou Hidden Love of God	414				
Thy Holy Wings, O Savior	502				
Your Love, O God, Has Called Us Here	647				
We Sing to You, O God				2001	
The Lily of the Valley				2062	

Scripture Hymn Title	UMH	MVPC	CLUW	TFWS	SOZ
Spirit of God				2117	
Shine, Jesus, Shine				2173	

1 Corinthians 12:1-11

	UMH	MVPC	CLUW	TFWS	SOZ
God of Change and Glory	114				
Many Gifts, One Spirit	114		212		
Spirit of Faith, Come Down	332		219		
Like the Murmur of the Dove's Song	544				
Christ, from Whom All Blessings Flow	550		250		
All Praise to Our Redeeming Lord	554				
Forward Through the Ages	555				
Blest Be the Dear Uniting Love	566		254		
One Bread, One Body	620	324	237		
Holy Spirit, Come to Us				2118	
We Are the Body of Christ				2227	
We Are One in Christ Jesus				2229	
As a Fire Is Meant for Burning				2237	
We All Are One in Mission				2243	
Within the Day-to-Day				2245	

John 2:1-11

	UMH	MVPC	CLUW	TFWS	SOZ
Come, My Way, My Truth, My Life	164				
Blessed Jesus, at Thy Word	596		108		
Now the Silence	619				
Become to Us the Living Bread	630				
Fill My Cup, Lord	641				
As Man and Woman We Were Made	642				
Jesus, Joy of Our Desiring	644		344		
Your Love, O God, Has Called Us Here	647				

January 21, 2007 (Third Sunday after Epiphany)

Scripture Hymn Title	UMH	MVPC	CLUW	TFWS	SOZ
Nehemiah 8:1-3, 5-6, 8-10					
Blessed Be the Name	63				
O Word of God Incarnate	598				
Wonderful Words of Life	600	313			
Sing Them over Again to Me	600	313			
Come, Holy Ghost, Our Hearts Inspire	603		218		
This Is the Day, This Is the Day	657				
God Is Here	660				
Stand Up and Bless the Lord	662		128		
All Who Hunger				2126	
You Who Are Thirsty				2132	
He Has Made Me Glad				2270	
Come! Come! Everybody Worship				2271	
The Trees of the Field				2279	
Psalm 19					
Holy, Holy, Holy! Lord God Almighty	64	4	79		
O Lord My God! When I in Awesome Wonder	77	2	61		
How Great Thou Art	77	2	61		
From All That Dwell Below the Skies	101		126		
This Is My Father's World	144	47	62		
Cantemos al Señor	149	49	67		
Let's Sing unto the Lord	149	49	67		
God, Who Stretched the Spangled Heavens	150		64		
God Created Heaven and Earth	151				
Jesus Shall Reign Where'er the Sun	157				
Alleluia	186		355		

Scripture Hymn Title	UMH	MVPC	CLUW	TFWS	SOZ
O Crucified Redeemer	425				
Sing Them over Again to Me	600	313			
Wonderful Words of Life	600	313			
Thy Word Is a Lamp unto My Feet	601		109		
This Is the Day the Lord Hath Made	658				
Now, on Land and Sea Descending	685		372		
I Will Call upon the Lord				2002	
Praise the Source of Faith and Learning				2004	
Let All Things Now Living				2008	
We Sing of Your Glory				2011	
Let Us with a Joyful Mind				2012	
Great Is the Lord				2022	
As the Deer				2025	
Awesome God				2040	
More Precious than Silver				2065	
Praise the Name of Jesus				2066	
I Love You, Lord				2068	
To Know You More				2161	
My Life Flows On				2212	

1 Corinthians 12:12-31*a*

Scripture Hymn Title	UMH	MVPC	CLUW	TFWS	SOZ
O For a Thousand Tongues to Sing	57	1	226		
Mil Voces Para Celebrar	59				
Many Gifts, One Spirit	114		212		
God of Change and Glory	114		212		
Like the Murmur of the Dove's Song	544				
O Church of God, United	547		249		
In Christ There Is No East or West	548				65
Where Charity and Love Prevail	549				
Christ, from Whom All Blessings Flow	550		250		
All Praise to Our Redeeming Lord	554				
Jesus, United by Thy Grace	561				
Break Thou the Bread of Life	599				
We Know That Christ Is Raised	610		231		
One Bread, One Body	620	324	237		
Together We Serve				2175	
We Need a Faith				2181	
We Are God's People				2220	

Scripture Hymn Title	UMH	MVPC	CLUW	TFWS	SOZ
In Unity We Lift Our Song				2221	
They'll Know We Are Christians by Our Love				2223	
Make Us One				2224	
Who Is My Mother, Who Is My Brother				2225	
We Are the Body of Christ				2227	
We Are One in Christ Jesus				2229	
Come Now, O Prince of Peace				2232	
As a Fire Is Meant for Burning				2237	
One God and Father of Us All				2240	
We All Are One in Mission				2243	
Within the Day-to-Day				2245	
Come, Be Baptized				2252	

Luke 4:14-21

Scripture Hymn Title	UMH	MVPC	CLUW	TFWS	SOZ
O For a Thousand Tongues to Sing	57	1	226		
Mil Voces Para Celebrar	59				
Jesus Shall Reign Where'er the Sun	157				
Morning Glory, Starlit Sky	194				
When Jesus the Healer Passed Through Galilee	263		171		
Spirit of Faith, Come Down	332		219		
Come, Ye Sinners, Poor and Needy	340				
Come, All of You	350				
Open My Eyes, That I May See	454	184			
Break Thou the Bread of Life	599				
Holy				2019	
The King of Glory Comes				2091	
Holy Spirit, Come to Us				2118	
The Summons				2130	
We Are Called				2172	
The Spirit Sends Us Forth to Serve				2241	

January 28, 2007 (Fourth Sunday after Epiphany)

Scripture Hymn Title	UMH	MVPC	CLUW	TFWS	SOZ
Jeremiah 1:4-10					
Morning Glory, Starlit Sky	194				
Of All the Spirit's Gifts to Me	336				
O Master, Let Me Walk with Thee	430		315		
Lord, Speak to Me, That I May Speak	463				
Send Me, Lord	497		331		
Whom Shall I Send?	582				
Here I Am, Lord	593	289	263		
I, the Lord of Sea and Sky	593	289	263		
How Shall They Hear the Word of God	649				
Womb of Life				2046	
Mothering God, You Gave Me Birth				2050	
I Was There to Hear Your Borning Cry				2051	
The Lone, Wild Bird				2052	
Spirit of God				2117	
Loving Spirit				2123	
Oh, I Know the Lord's Laid His Hands on Me				2139	
We Are Called				2172	
Psalm 71:1-6					
Now Thank We All Our God	102				
A Mighty Fortress Is Our God	110	25			
O God, Our Help in Ages Past	117				
All My Hope Is Firmly Grounded	132				
Leaning on the Everlasting Arms	133	244	291		53
What a Fellowship, What a Joy Divine	133	244	291		53
Praise to the Lord, the Almighty	139	29	68		
Rock of Ages, Cleft for Me	361	247			

Scripture Hymn Title	UMH	MVPC	CLUW	TFWS	SOZ
Saranam, Saranam	523		105		
Jesus, Savior, Lord, Lo, to Thee I Fly	523		105		
We Sing to You, O God				2001	
I Will Call Upon the Lord				2002	
Praise You				2003	
My Life Is in You, Lord				2032	
Mothering God, You Gave Me Birth				2050	
I Was there to Hear Your Borning Cry				2051	
Praise the Name of Jesus				2066	
Lord of All Hopefulness				2197	

1 Corinthians 13:1-13

Scripture Hymn Title	UMH	MVPC	CLUW	TFWS	SOZ
Morning Glory, Starlit Sky	194				
The Gift of Love	408		341		
Though I May Speak with Bravest Fire	408		341		
Come Down, O Love Divine	475				
We Are Tossed and Driven on the Restless Sea of Time	525	317			
We'll Understand It Better By and By	525	317			55
Now the Silence	619				
As Man and Woman We Were Made	642				
When Love Is Found	643		343		
O Perfect Love, All Human Thought Transcending	645				
Canticle of Love	646				
Live in Charity				2179	
Sacred the Body				2228	
Gather Us In				2236	

Luke 4:21-30

Scripture Hymn Title	UMH	MVPC	CLUW	TFWS	SOZ
I Danced in the Morning	261	128	170		
Lord of the Dance	261	128	170		
O Young and Fearless Prophet	444				
In Christ There Is No East or West	548				65
Christ for the World We Sing	568	260			
Now Praise the Hidden God of Love				2027	
Spirit, Spirit of Gentleness				2120	

February 4, 2007 (Fifth Sunday after Epiphany)

Scripture Hymn Title	UMH	MVPC	CLUW	TFWS	SOZ
Isaiah 6:1-13					
Holy, Holy, Holy! Lord God Almighty	64	4	79		
¡Santo! ¡Santo! ¡Santo!	65				
Holy God, We Praise Thy Name	79		80		
Canticle of the Holy Trinity, Response	80				
Ye Watchers and Ye Holy Ones	90				
The God of Abraham Praise	116	28			
Psalm 24 (King James Version)	212				
We Would See Jesus	256		168		
The Voice of God Is Calling	436		139		
Send Me, Lord	497		331		
Faith, While Trees Are Still in Blossom	508		97		
Whom Shall I Send?	582				
Here I Am, Lord	593	289	263		
I, the Lord of Sea and Sky	593	289	263		
Let All Mortal Flesh Keep Silence	626		150		217
Stand Up and Bless the Lord	662		128		
Day Is Dying in the West	687				
Holy, Holy, Holy				2007	
Honor and Praise				2018	
Holy				2019	
Holy, Holy				2039	
Holy, Holy, Holy Lord				2256	
Holy Ground				2272	
Psalm 138					
The Lord's My Shepherd, I'll Not Want	136		115		
The King of Love My Shepherd Is	138				
Great Is Thy Faithfulness	140	30	81		

Scripture	Hymn Title	UMH	MVPC	CLUW	TFWS	SOZ
	O God Beyond All Praising				2009	
	Give Thanks				2036	
	You Are My Hiding Place				2055	
	Praise Our God Above				2061	
	Thank You, Jesus				2081	
	Someone Asked the Question				2144	
	He Who Began a Good Work in You				2163	
	In the Lord I'll Be Ever Thankful				2195	
	The Fragrance of Christ				2205	

1 Corinthians 15:1-11

Scripture	Hymn Title	UMH	MVPC	CLUW	TFWS	SOZ
	There Is a Name I Love to Hear	170		198		36
	O How I Love Jesus	170		198		36
	He Is Lord, He Is Lord	177	173			233
	Christ the Lord Is Risen Today	302	152	193		
	The Day of Resurrection	303		188		
	Easter People, Raise Your Voices	304				6
	The Strife Is O'er, the Battle Done	306				
	Christ Is Risen! Shout Hosanna!	307				
	I Serve a Risen Savior	310	149			30
	He Lives	310	149			30
	Now the Green Blade Riseth	311				
	Christ Is Risen, Christ Is Living	313				
	Cristo Vive, Fuera El Llanto	313				
	O Sons and Daughters, Let Us Sing	317				
	And Can It Be that I Should Gain	363	206	280		
	Amazing Grace! How Sweet the Sound	378	203	94		211
	Come, Thou Fount of Every Blessing	400	42	127		
	The Voice of God Is Calling	436		139		
	Sing with All the Saints in Glory	702		382		
	Amen, Amen				2072	
	Shout to the Lord				2074	
	Lord, I Lift Your Name on High				2088	
	Christ Has Risen				2115	
	Christ the Lord Is Risen				2116	
	Grace Alone				2162	

Scripture Hymn Title	UMH	MVPC	CLUW	TFWS	SOZ

Luke 5:1-11

	UMH	MVPC	CLUW	TFWS	SOZ
I Danced in the Morning	261	128	170		
Lord of the Dance	261	128	170		
I Can Hear My Savior Calling	338				42
Where He Leads Me	338				42
Lord, You Have Come to the Lakeshore	344	195	90		
Tú Has Venido a la Orilla	344	195	90		
Dear Lord and Father of Mankind	358				
Jesus Calls Us O'er the Tumult	398		96		
O Master, Let Me Walk with Thee	430		315		
Forth in Thy Name, O Lord, I Go	438				
Faith, While Trees Are Still in Blossom	508		97		
Rise Up, O Men of God	576				
Here I Am, Lord	593	289	263		
I, the Lord of Sea and Sky	593	289	263		
Rise Up, Shepherd, and Follow				2096	
Two Fishermen				2101	
I Have Decided to Follow Jesus				2129	
The Summons				2130	
Would I Have Answered When You Called				2137	
You Are Mine				2218	

February 11, 2007 (Sixth Sunday after Epiphany)

Scripture Hymn Title	UMH	MVPC	CLUW	TFWS	SOZ
Jeremiah 17:5-10					
Seek the Lord Who Now Is Present	124				
All My Hope Is Firmly Grounded	132				
If Thou But Suffer God to Guide Thee	142				
Come, Every Soul by Sin Oppressed	337				
Only Trust Him	337				
O For a Heart to Praise My God	417				
Make Me a Captive, Lord	421				
Trust and Obey	467		320		
When We Walk with the Lord	467		320		
Through It All	507		279		
Be Still, My Soul	534		307		
O Day of God, Draw Nigh	730				
Come, We That Love the Lord (St. Thomas)	732				
Come, We That Love the Lord (Marching to Zion)	733				3
We're Marching to Zion	733				3
The First Song of Isaiah				2030	
My Life Is in You, Lord				2032	
The Lone, Wild Bird				2052	
Nothing Can Trouble				2054	
Praise the Name of Jesus				2066	
Guide My Feet				2208	
Lead Me, Guide Me				2214	
Cares Chorus				2215	
Psalm 1					
Righteous and Just Is the Word of Our Lord	107				

Scripture Hymn Title	UMH	MVPC	CLUW	TFWS	SOZ
La Palabra Del Señor Es Recta	107				
Seek the Lord Who Now Is Present	124				
All My Hope Is Firmly Grounded	132				
If Thou But Suffer God to Guide Thee	142				
On Eagle's Wings	143		83		
A Charge to Keep I Have	413				
Through It All	507		279		
Blessed Jesus, at Thy Word	596		108		
O Word of God Incarnate	598				
Thy Word Is a Lamp unto My Feet	601		109		
Praise the Source of Faith and Learning				2004	
The First Song of Isaiah				2030	
My Life Is in You, Lord				2032	
The Lone, Wild Bird				2052	
Nothing Can Trouble				2054	
Praise the Name of Jesus				2066	
O Blessed Spring				2076	
Love the Lord Your God				2168	
Guide My Feet				2208	
Lead Me, Guide Me				2214	

1 Corinthians 15:12-20

Scripture Hymn Title	UMH	MVPC	CLUW	TFWS	SOZ
There Is a Name I Love to Hear	170		198		
O How I Love Jesus	170		198		36
Hope of the World	178				
Christ the Lord Is Risen Today	302	152	193		
I Serve a Risen Savior	310	149			30
He Lives	310				30
Cristo Vive, Fuera El Llanto	313				
Christ Is Risen, Christ Is Living	313				
Because He Lives	364	154	285		
This Is a Day of New Beginnings	383	208	311		
A Charge to Keep I Have	413				
We Know That Christ Is Raised	610		231		
Sing with All the Saints in Glory	702		382		
Alleluia (Celtic)				2043	
Christ the Lord Is Risen				2116	

Scripture Hymn Title	UMH	MVPC	CLUW	TFWS	SOZ
Luke 6:17-26					
Come, Every Soul by Sin Oppressed	337				
Only Trust Him	337				
Jesus Calls Us o'er the Tumult	398		96		
Lord, I Want to Be a Christian	402	215			76
I Want a Principle Within	410				
Make Me a Captive, Lord	421				
When We Walk with the Lord	467		320		
Trust and Obey	467		320		
Through It All	507		279		
Am I a Soldier of the Cross	511				
How Firm a Foundation	529	256			
Praise, My Soul, the King of Heaven	66				
Rejoice in God's Saints	708				
I Sing a Song of the Saints of God	712				
O Day of God, Draw Nigh	730				
Come, We That Love the Lord (St. Thomas)	732				
Holy				2019	
Give Thanks				2036	
Blest Are They				2155	
Goodness Is Stronger than Evil				2219	
For All the Saints				2283	

February 18, 2007 (Transfiguration Sunday)

Scripture Hymn Title	UMH	MVPC	CLUW	TFWS	SOZ
Exodus 34:29-35					
Immortal, Invisible, God Only Wise	103		74		
God Created Heaven and Earth	151				
When Morning Gilds the Skies	185		369		
O Wondrous Sight! O Vision Fair	258		169		
Be Thou My Vision	451	240			
God the Spirit, Guide and Guardian	648				
Come, Holy Ghost, Our Souls Inspire	651				
Gloria, Gloria in Excelsis Deo! *(canon)*	72		353		
You Alone Are Holy				2077	
Holy Ground				2272	
Psalm 99					
Immortal, Invisible, God Only Wise	103		74		
La Palabra Del Señor Es Recta	107				
Righteous and Just Is the Word of Our Lord	107				
El Shaddai	123	45	77		
Praise to the Lord, the Almighty	139	29	68		
Lift High the Cross	159	164	174		
Crown Him with Many Crowns	327	157			
Praise, My Soul, the King of Heaven	66				
O Worship the King, All-Glorious Above	73				
How Great Thou Art	77	2	61		
O Lord My God! When I in Awesome Wonder	77	2	61		
Holy God, We Praise Thy Name	79		80		
Praise the Lord Who Reigns Above	96		124		
Holy, Holy, Holy				2007	

Scripture Hymn Title	UMH	MVPC	CLUW	TFWS	SOZ
O God Beyond All Praising				2009	
Honor and Praise				2018	
Glory to God				2033	
Awesome God				2040	
All Hail King Jesus				2069	
He Is Exalted				2070	
We Will Glorify the King of Kings				2087	
Lord, Be Glorified				2150	
Wounded World that Cries for Healing				2177	
Unsettled World				2183	
He Has Made Me Glad				2270	

2 Corinthians 3:12–4:2

Scripture Hymn Title	UMH	MVPC	CLUW	TFWS	SOZ
O Wondrous Sight! O Vision Fair	258		169		
Spirit of Faith, Come Down	332		219		
Depth of Mercy! Can There Be	355		273		
Love Divine, All Loves Excelling	384				
O Come and Dwell in Me	388				
Take Time to Be Holy	395				
O Jesus, I Have Promised	396	214			
Come, Thou Fount of Every Blessing	400	42	127		
For the Healing of the Nations	428				
Blessed Jesus, at Thy Word	596		108		
Come, Holy Ghost, Our Hearts Inspire	603		218		
Where the Spirit of the Lord Is				2119	
Change My Heart, O God				2152	
Shine, Jesus, Shine				2173	

Luke 9:28-43

Scripture Hymn Title	UMH	MVPC	CLUW	TFWS	SOZ
I Love to Tell the Story	156	56			
Christ, Whose Glory Fills the Skies	173		281		
Majesty, Worship His Majesty	176	171	204		
When Morning Gilds the Skies	185		369		
Christ Is the World's Light	188				
Jesus! the Name High over All	193		199		
O Wondrous Sight! O Vision Fair	258		169		
Christ, upon the Mountain Peak	260				
Silence, Frenzied, Unclean Spirit	264				

Scripture	Hymn Title	UMH	MVPC	CLUW	TFWS	SOZ
	O Christ, the Healer, We Have Come	265				
	Turn Your Eyes upon Jesus	349				
	Take Time to Be Holy	395				
	O Jesus, I Have Promised	396	214			
	Where Cross the Crowded Ways of Life	427	296			
	Be Thou My Vision	451	240			
	Dear Lord, for All in Pain	458				
	I Come with Joy to Meet My Lord	617				
	Here, O My Lord, I See Thee	623				
	Honor and Praise				2018	
	All Hail King Jesus				2069	
	He Is Exalted				2070	
	Swiftly Pass the Clouds of Glory				2102	
	We Have Come at Christ's Own Bidding				2103	
	Come Away with Me				2202	
	Holy Ground				2272	

February 21, 2007 (Ash Wednesday)

Scripture	Hymn Title	UMH	MVPC	CLUW	TFWS	SOZ
Joel 2:1-2, 12-17						
	There's a Wideness in God's Mercy	121				
	Sing, My Tongue, the Glorious Battle	296				
	Blow Ye the Trumpet, Blow	379	309			
	Lord, I Want to Be a Christian	402	215			76
	All Who Love and Serve Your City	433				
	Weary of All Trumpeting	442				
	See How Great a Flame Aspires	541		248		
	My Lord, What a Morning	719		386		145
	Forgive Us, Lord				2134	
	Sanctuary				2164	
	Without Seeing You				2206	
Psalm 51:1-17						
	O For a Thousand Tongues to Sing	57	1	226		
	Mil Voces Para Celebrar	59				
	Pass Me Not, O Gentle Savior	351		271		
	Depth of Mercy! Can There Be	355		273		
	Just As I Am, Without One Plea	357				208
	Have Thine Own Way, Lord!	382	213	327		
	I Want a Principle Within	410				
	O For a Heart to Praise My God	417				
	Breathe on Me, Breath of God	420				
	Open My Eyes, That I May See	454	184			
	Jesus, Lover of My Soul	479				
	Thy Holy Wings, O Savior	502				
	Bread of the World in Mercy Broken	624		240		
	Come, Rejoice in God				2017	
	Open Our Eyes				2086	
	Give Me a Clean Heart				2133	

Scripture	Hymn Title	UMH	MVPC	CLUW	TFWS	SOZ
	Forgive Us, Lord				2134	
	Sunday's Palms Are Wednesday's Ashes				2138	
	Since Jesus Came Into My Heart				2140	
	Change My Heart, O God				2152	
	Please Enter My Heart, Hosanna				2154	
	Come and Fill Our Hearts				2157	
	Just a Closer Walk with Thee				2158	
	Kyrie				2275	
	Lord, Have Mercy				2277	

2 Corinthians 5:20*b*–6:10

Scripture	Hymn Title	UMH	MVPC	CLUW	TFWS	SOZ
	In Thee Is Gladness	169				
	Ye Servants of God, Your Master Proclaim	181				
	Morning Glory, Starlit Sky	194				
	What Wondrous Love Is This	292				
	Alas! and Did My Savior Bleed	294				8
	Come, Every Soul by Sin Oppressed	337				
	Only Trust Him	337				
	Come Back Quickly to the Lord	343		272		
	Depth of Mercy! Can There Be	355		273		
	Alas! and Did My Savior Bleed	359	202			8
	Love Divine, All Loves Excelling	384				
	Let Us Plead for Faith Alone	385				
	Close to Thee	407				7
	Thou My Everlasting Portion	407				7
	I Want a Principle Within	410				
	O For a Heart to Praise My God	417				
	Creator of the Earth and Skies	450				
	Holy Spirit, Truth Divine	465				
	Spirit of God, Descend upon My Heart	500				
	Stand Up, Stand Up for Jesus	514				
	There Are Some Things I May Not Know				2147	
	Cry of My Heart				2165	
	More Like You				2167	
	We Walk by Faith				2196	
	Lead On, O Cloud of Presence				2234	
	In the Singing				2255	

Scripture Hymn Title	UMH	MVPC	CLUW	TFWS	SOZ
Matthew 6:1-6, 16-21					
Lord, Who Throughout these Forty Days	269		181		
He Never Said a Mumbalin' Word	291				101
Daw-Kee, Aim Daw-Tsi-Taw	330				
It's Me, It's Me, O Lord	352		326		110
Standing in the Need of Prayer	352		326		110
Just As I Am, Without One Plea	357				208
Love Divine, All Loves Excelling	384				
Let Us Plead for Faith Alone	385				
Take Time to Be Holy	395				
Lord, I Want to Be a Christian	402	215			76
More Love to Thee, O Christ	453		318		
Near to the Heart of God	472		324		
There Is a Place of Quiet Rest	472		324		
Prayer Is the Soul's Sincere Desire	492				
Sweet Hour of Prayer	496	248	330		
Serenity	499				
O Sabbath Rest of Galilee	499				
Come and Find the Quiet Center				2128	
Sunday's Palms Are Wednesday's Ashes				2138	
Since Jesus Came into My Heart				2140	
I'm So Glad Jesus Lifted Me				2151	
God, How Can We Forgive				2169	
Prayers of the People				2201	
Come Away with Me				2202	
The Fragrance of Christ				2205	
Jesus, We Are Here				2273	

February 25, 2007 (First Sunday in Lent)

Scripture Hymn Title	UMH	MVPC	CLUW	TFWS	SOZ
Deuteronomy 26:1-11					
Praise, My Soul, the King of Heaven	66				
What Gift Can We Bring	87				
For the Fruits of This Creation	97				
God, Whose Love Is Reigning o'er Us	100		73		
The God of Abraham Praise	116	28			
Praise to the Lord, the Almighty	139	29	68		
Come, Ye Thankful People, Come	694		241		
God of the Ages	698	377			
O God Beyond All Praising				2009	
How Majestic Is Your Name				2023	
We Bring the Sacrifice of Praise				2031	
Lead On, O Cloud of Presence				2234	
In the Midst of New Dimensions				2238	
Psalm 91:1-2, 9-16					
A Mighty Fortress Is Our God	110	25			
O God, Our Help in Ages Past	117				
Be Not Dismayed Whate'er Betide	130				
God Will Take Care of You	130	260			
Children of the Heavenly Father	141		335		
On Eagle's Wings	143		83		
When Peace, Like a River, Attendeth My Way	377	250	304		20
It Is Well with My Soul	377	250	304		20
Dear Lord, Lead Me Day by Day	411		100		
I Will Trust in the Lord	464		292		14
By Gracious Powers So Wonderfully Sheltered	517				

Scripture	Hymn Title	UMH	MVPC	CLUW	TFWS	SOZ
	Saranam, Saranam	523		105		
	Jesus, Savior, Lord, Lo, to Thee I Fly	523				
	Nothing Can Trouble				2054	
	Praise the Name of Jesus				2066	
	Shout to the Lord				2074	
	Holy Spirit, Come to Us				2118	

Romans 10:8b-13

	At the Name of Jesus Every Knee Shall Bow	168				
	He Is Lord, He Is Lord	177	173			233
	Let Us Plead for Faith Alone	385				
	I Know Not Why God's Wondrous Grace	714		290		
	I Know Whom I Have Believed	714		290		
	I Will Call upon the Lord				2002	
	O God Beyond All Praising				2009	
	Since Jesus Came into My Heart				2140	
	Into My Heart				2160	

Luke 4:1-13

	Hope of the World	178				
	When Jesus Came to Jordan	252	125			
	We Meet You, O Christ	257				
	O Love, How Deep, How Broad, How High	267				
	Lord, Who Throughout These Forty Days	269		181		
	Take Time to Be Holy	395				
	Seek Ye First the Kingdom of God	405	201	136		
	I Want a Principle Within	410				
	Dear Jesus, in Whose Life I See	468				
	Jesus, Tempted in the Desert				2105	
	Jesus Walked This Lonesome Valley				2112	
	Faith Is Patience in the Night				2211	

March 4, 2007 (Second Sunday in Lent)

Scripture Hymn Title	UMH	MVPC	CLUW	TFWS	SOZ
Genesis 15:1-12, 17-18					
God, Whose Love Is Reigning o'er Us	100		73		
The God of Abraham Praise	116	28			
El Shaddai	123	45	77		
All My Hope Is Firmly Grounded	132				
Great Is Thy Faithfulness	140	30	81		
If Thou But Suffer God to Guide Thee	142				
Faith, While Trees Are Still in Blossom	508		97		
Come Away with Me				2202	
Psalm 27					
O God, Our Help in Ages Past	117				
Guide Me, O Thou Great Jehovah	127 ✓				
Give to the Winds Thy Fears	129		282		
Thou Hidden Source of Calm Repose	153		346		
I Sought the Lord, and Afterward I Knew	341				
Rock of Ages, Cleft for Me	361	247			
Jesus, Lover of My Soul	479				
My Prayer Rises to Heaven	498				
Thy Holy Wings, O Savior	502				
O Thou, in Whose Presence My Soul Takes Delight	518				
Saranam, Saranam	523		105		
Jesus, Savior, Lord, Lo, to Thee I Fly	523		105		
I Love Thy Kingdom, Lord	540				
God of Grace and God of Glory	577	287			
Lead On, O King Eternal	580	174			
Here, O My Lord, I See Thee	623				
Sing with All the Saints in Glory	702		382		

Scripture Hymn Title	UMH	MVPC	CLUW	TFWS	SOZ
Soon and Very Soon	706		385		198
I Will Call upon the Lord				2002	
If It Had Not Been for the Lord				2053	
Nothing Can Trouble				2054	
You Are My Hiding Place				2055	
O Lord, You're Beautiful				2064	
Shout to the Lord				2074	
Someone Asked the Question				2144	
Cry of My Heart				2165	
We Are Called				2172	
Shine, Jesus, Shine				2173	
Lord, Listen to Your Children				2207	
Lead Me, Guide Me				2214	
You Are Mine				2218	
We Are Singing/We Are Marching/SIYAHAMBA				2235a-b	
Taste and See				2267	

Philippians 3:17–4:1

Scripture Hymn Title	UMH	MVPC	CLUW	TFWS	SOZ
O Sacred Head, Now Wounded	286	139			
O Jesus, I Have Promised	396	214			
O For a Heart to Praise My God	417				
I Am Thine, O Lord	419	218			
Stand Up, Stand Up for Jesus	514				
By Gracious Powers So Wonderfully Sheltered	517				
Beams of Heaven as I Go	524				10, 207
Lead On, O King Eternal	580	174			
Stand Up and Bless the Lord	662		128		

Luke 13:31-35

Scripture Hymn Title	UMH	MVPC	CLUW	TFWS	SOZ
Holy, Holy, Holy! Lord God Almighty	64	4	79		
God of Many Names	105				
God Hath Spoken by the Prophets	108	38			
How Like a Gentle Spirit	115		216		
The Care the Eagle Gives Her Young	118		302		
Children of the Heavenly Father	141		335		
I Danced in the Morning	261	128	170		
Lord of the Dance	261	128	170		

Scripture Hymn Title	UMH	MVPC	CLUW	TFWS	SOZ
O Love, How Deep, How Broad, How High	267				
Softly and Tenderly Jesus Is Calling	348	193	284		
By Gracious Powers So Wonderfully Sheltered	517				
Jesus, Savior, Lord, Lo, to Thee I Fly	523		105		
Saranam, Saranam	523		105		
Beams of Heaven as I Go	524				10, 207
We Sing to You, O God				2001	
Holy, Holy, Holy				2007	
Blessed Be the Name of the Lord				2034	
Jesus Walked This Lonesome Valley				2112	
Loving Spirit				2123	
Come Away with Me				2202	

March 11, 2007 (Third Sunday in Lent)

Scripture Hymn Title	UMH	MVPC	CLUW	TFWS	SOZ
Isaiah 55:1-9					
There's a Wideness in God's Mercy	121				
Seek the Lord Who Now Is Present	124				
Canticle of Covenant Faithfulness	125				
Come, Sinners, to the Gospel Feast (Invitation)	339	88			
Come, Ye Sinners, Poor and Needy	340				
Come, All of You	350				
Just as I Am, Without One Plea	357				208
All Who Love and Serve Your City	433				
Come, Ye Disconsolate, Where'er Ye Languish	510				
Come, Sinners, to the Gospel Feast (Communion)	616				
You Satisfy the Hungry Heart	629				
O God Beyond All Praising				2009	
You Who Are Thirsty				2132	
We Walk by Faith				2196	
Gather Us In				2236	
I'll Fly Away				2282	
Psalm 63:1-8					
On Eagle's Wings	143	83			
Savior, Like a Shepherd Lead Us	381				
Be Thou My Vision	451	240			
Come Down, O Love Divine	475				
My Prayer Rises to Heaven	498				
Wellspring of Wisdom	506				
O Food to Pilgrims Given	631				
As the Deer				2025	

Scripture Hymn Title	UMH	MVPC	CLUW	TFWS	SOZ
Praise the Name of Jesus				2066	
Spirit of God				2117	
Someone Asked the Question				2144	
When We Are Called to Sing Your Praise				2216	

1 Corinthians 10:1-13

	UMH	MVPC	CLUW	TFWS	SOZ
Guide Me, O Thou Great Jehovah	127				
Lord, Who Throughout These Forty Days	269		181		
Rock of Ages, Cleft for Me	361	247			
O Jesus, I Have Promised	396	214			
I Want a Principle Within	410				
A Charge to Keep I Have	413				
Come Out the Wilderness	416				136
I Am Leaning on the Lord	416				136
Make Me a Captive, Lord	421				
Lead Me, Lord	473				
Wellspring of Wisdom	506				
Lift Every Voice and Sing	519				32
How Shall They Hear the Word of God	649				
Glorious Things of Thee Are Spoken	731		256		
We Sing to You, O God				2001	
Praise the Name of Jesus				2066	

Luke 13:1-9

	UMH	MVPC	CLUW	TFWS	SOZ
Softly and Tenderly Jesus Is Calling	348	193	284		
A Charge to Keep I Have	413				
I Am Leaning on the Lord	416				136
Come Out the Wilderness	416				136
Forth in Thy Name, O Lord, I Go	438				
Wellspring of Wisdom	506				
Lift Every Voice and Sing	519				32
O Zion, Haste	573				
Lord, Whose Love Through Humble Service	581				
Sois la Semilla	583	291			
You Are the Seed	583	291			

Scripture Hymn Title	UMH	MVPC	CLUW	TFWS	SOZ
When the Church of Jesus Shuts Its Outer Door	592				
Lord, Dismiss Us with Thy Blessing	671				
Come, We That Love the Lord (St. Thomas)	732				
Come, We That Love the Lord (Marching to Zion)	733				3
We're Marching to Zion	733				3
God the Sculptor of the Mountains				2060	

March 18, 2007 (Fourth Sunday in Lent)

Scripture Hymn Title	UMH	MVPC	CLUW	TFWS	SOZ
Joshua 5:9-12					
For the Fruits of This Creation	97				
All My Hope Is Firmly Grounded	132				
The King of Love My Shepherd Is	138				
O Food to Pilgrims Given	631				
God of the Ages	698	377			
Psalm 32					
Seek the Lord Who Now Is Present	124				
Canticle of Covenant Faithfulness	125				
Great Is Thy Faithfulness	140	30	81		
Rejoice, Ye Pure in Heart (Marion)	160		130		
Rejoice, Ye Pure in Heart (Vineyard Haven)	161				
Depth of Mercy! Can There Be	355		273		
Grace Greater than Our Sin	365				
Amazing Grace! How Sweet the Sound	378	203	94		211
O Happy Day, That Fixed My Choice	391				
Through It All	507		279		
Out of the Depths I Cry to You	515				
My Life Is in You, Lord				2032	
If It Had Not Been for the Lord				2053	
You Are My Hiding Place				2055	
Forgive Us, Lord				2134	
Cry of My Heart				2165	
Healer of Our Every Ill				2213	
Taste and See				2267	
He Has Made Me Glad				2270	
The Trees of the Field				2279	

Scripture Hymn Title	UMH	MVPC	CLUW	TFWS	SOZ
2 Corinthians 5:16-21					
What Wondrous Love Is This	292				
Alas! and Did My Savior Bleed	294				8
Camina, Pueblo De Dios	305	151			
Walk On, O People of God	305				
Alas! and Did My Savior Bleed	359	202			8
This Is a Day of New Beginnings	383	208	311		
Love Divine, All Loves Excelling	384				
O Come and Dwell in Me	388				
The Church's One Foundation	545	269	255		
Christ for the World We Sing	568		260		
O Zion, Haste	573				
Lord God, Your Love Has Called Us Here	579				
We Know That Christ Is Raised	610		231		
Womb of Life				2046	
Mothering God, You Gave Me Birth				2050	
Change My Heart, O God				2152	
Come Now, O Prince of Peace				2232	
Luke 15:1-3, 11*b*-32					
How Like a Gentle Spirit	115		216		
Your Love, O God	120	26			
God of the Sparrow God of the Whale	122	37	59		
Come, Sinners, to the Gospel Feast (Invitation)	339		88		
Come, Ye Sinners, Poor and Needy	340				
Come Back Quickly to the Lord	343		272		
Softly and Tenderly Jesus Is Calling	348	193	284		
Just as I Am, Without One Plea	357				208
Amazing Grace! How Sweet the Sound	378	203	94		211
Love Divine, All Loves Excelling	384				
Cuando El Pobre Nada Tiene	434	301	138		
When the Poor Ones Who Have Nothing	434	301	138		
O God Who Shaped Creation	443				
Through It All	507		279		
Come, Sinners, to the Gospel Feast (Communion)	616				

Scripture Hymn Title	UMH	MVPC	CLUW	TFWS	SOZ
Now the Silence	619				
Canticle of Love	646				
Bring Many Names				2047	
Mothering God, You Gave Me Birth				2050	
If It Had Not Been for the Lord				2053	
You Are My Hiding Place				2055	
Forgive Us, Lord				2134	
Sunday's Palms Are Wednesday's Ashes				2138	
Living for Jesus				2149	
I'm So Glad Jesus Lifted Me				2151	
Please Enter My Heart, Hosanna				2154	
Lord of All Hopefulness				2197	
Lead Me, Guide Me				2214	

March 25, 2007 (Fifth Sunday in Lent)

Scripture Hymn Title	UMH	MVPC	CLUW	TFWS	SOZ
Isaiah 43:16-21					
Sing Praise to God Who Reigns Above	126		60		
O Mary, Don't You Weep, Don't You Mourn	134				153
Cantemos al Señor	149	49	67		
Let's Sing unto the Lord	149	49	67		
This Is a Day of New Beginnings	383	208	311		
O Come and Dwell in Me	388				
Go Down, Moses	448				112
Wellspring of Wisdom	506				
Jesus, Savior, Pilot Me	509				49
Out of the Depths I Cry to You	515				
Psalm 126					
O God, Our Help in Ages Past	117				
Give to the Winds Thy Fears	129		282		
Cantemos al Señor	149	49	67		
Let's Sing unto the Lord	149	49	67		
Rejoice, Ye Pure in Heart (Marion)	160		130		
Rejoice, Ye Pure in Heart (Vineyard Haven)	161				
Hail to the Lord's Anointed	203	81			
Come, Ye Disconsolate, Where'er Ye Languish	510				
O Spirit of the Living God	539				
Bless His Holy Name				2015	
When God Restored Our Common Life				2182	
Joy Comes with the Dawn				2210	

Scripture Hymn Title	UMH	MVPC	CLUW	TFWS	SOZ
Philippians 3:4b-14					
Jesus, the Very Thought of Thee	175				
When I Survey the Wondrous Cross (Hamburg)	298	138			
When I Survey the Wondrous Cross (Rockingham)	299				
And Can It Be that I Should Gain	363	206	280		
My Hope Is Built on Nothing Less	368	261			
Standing on the Promises of Christ My King	374	252			
This Is a Day of New Beginnings	383	208	311		
O Come and Dwell in Me	388				
Something Beautiful, Something Good	394		303		
Jesus Calls Us O'er the Tumult	398		96		
Take My Life, and Let It Be Consecrated	399		312		
Thou My Everlasting Portion	407				7
Close to Thee	407				7
I Want a Principle Within	410				
A Charge to Keep I Have	413				
Thou Hidden Love of God	414				
Go Down, Moses	448				112
Be Thou My Vision	451	240			
More Love to Thee, O Christ	453		318		
When Our Confidence Is Shaken	505				
Nearer, My God, to Thee	528		308		
The Church's One Foundation	546				
The Church of Christ, in Every Age	589				
Sing the Wondrous Love of Jesus	701		381		15
Come, Let Us Join Our Friends Above	709		387		
My Song Is Love Unknown				2083	
To Know You More				2161	
Grace Alone				2162	
He Who Began a Good Work in You				2163	
Sanctuary				2164	
More Like You				2167	
Guide My Feet				2208	
Healer of Our Every Ill				2213	

Scripture Hymn Title	UMH	MVPC	CLUW	TFWS	SOZ
John 12:1-8					
There Is a Name I Love to Hear	170		198		36
O How I Love Jesus	170		198		36
My Jesus, I Love Thee	172		321		
Jesus, the Very Thought of Thee	175				
Morning Glory, Starlit Sky	194				
Prepare the Way of the Lord	207		141		
Woman in the Night	274				
The First One Ever, Oh, Ever to Know	276				
Something Beautiful, Something Good	394		303		
O Young and Fearless Prophet	444				
Jesus, Lord, We Look to Thee	562				
Cry of My Heart				2165	
When We Are Called to Sing Your Praise				2216	

April 1, 2007 (Palm/Passion Sunday)

Scripture Hymn Title	UMH	MVPC	CLUW	TFWS	SOZ
Liturgy of the Palms					
Luke 19:28-40					
Heleluyan, Heleluyan	78	39	354		
Come, Christians, Join to Sing	158				
Rejoice, Ye Pure in Heart (Marion)	160		130		
Rejoice, Ye Pure in Heart (Vineyard Haven)	161				
When Morning Gilds the Skies	185		369		
Tell Me the Stories of Jesus	277		177		
Hosanna, Loud Hosanna, the Little Children Sang	278				
Mantos Y Palmas Esparciendo	279	136	178		
Filled with Excitement, All the Happy Throng	279	136	178		
All Glory, Laud, and Honor	280				
Blessed Be the Name of the Lord				2034	
My Song Is Love Unknown				2083	
We Will Glorify the King of Kings				2087	
The King of Glory Comes				2091	
Thou Didst Leave Thy Throne				2100	
Hosanna! Hosanna!				2109	
We Sang Our Glad Hosannas				2111	
Sunday's Palms Are Wednesday's Ashes				2138	
Holy, Holy, Holy Lord				2256	
Psalm 118:1-2, 19-29					
Heleluyan, Heleluyan	78	39	354		
Good Christian Friends, Rejoice	224		155		

Scripture	Hymn Title	UMH	MVPC	CLUW	TFWS	SOZ
	Filled with Excitement, All the Happy Throng	279	136	178		
	Mantos Y Palmas Esparciendo	279	136	178		
	All Glory, Laud, and Honor	280				
	Christ Is Made the Sure Foundation	559				
	This Is the Day, This Is the Day (This Is the Day)	657				
	This Is the Day the Lord Hath Made	658				
	Blessed Be the Name of the Lord				2034	
	Thank You, Jesus				2081	
	Come, Let Us with Our Lord Arise				2084	
	The King of Glory Comes				2091	
	Hosanna! Hosanna!				2109	
	We Sang Our Glad Hosannas				2111	
	Holy, Holy, Holy Lord				2256	
	He Has Made Me Glad				2270	

Liturgy of the Passion

Isaiah 50:4-9*a*

Scripture	Hymn Title	UMH	MVPC	CLUW	TFWS	SOZ
	If Thou But Suffer God to Guide Thee	142				
	Morning Glory, Starlit Sky	194				
	O Sacred Head, Now Wounded	286	139			
	They Crucified My Lord	291				
	He Never Said a Mumbalin' Word	291				101
	Open My Eyes, That I May See	454	184			
	Lord, Speak to Me, That I May Speak	463				
	There Is a Place of Quiet Rest	472		324		
	Near to the Heart of God	472		324		
	Precious Lord, Take My Hand	474		309		179
	Nothing Can Trouble				2054	
	Come, Let Us with Our Lord Arise				2084	
	Open Our Eyes				2086	
	Cry of My Heart				2165	
	Goodness Is Stronger than Evil				2219	

Psalm 31:9-16

Scripture	Hymn Title	UMH	MVPC	CLUW	TFWS	SOZ
	O Sacred Head, Now Wounded	286	139			
	Lead Me, Lord	473				

Scripture Hymn Title	UMH	MVPC	CLUW	TFWS	SOZ
Precious Lord, Take My Hand	474		309		179
Stand By Me	512				41
When the Storms of Life Are Raging	512				41
By Gracious Powers So Wonderfully Sheltered	517				
Jesus, Savior, Lord, Lo, to Thee I Fly	523		105		
Saranam, Saranam	523		105		
Jesus Walked This Lonesome Valley				2112	
Lord, Listen to Your Children				2207	
How Long, O Lord				2209	
Cares Chorus				2215	
You Are Mine				2218	

Philippians 2:5-11

Scripture Hymn Title	UMH	MVPC	CLUW	TFWS	SOZ
All Hail the Power of Jesus' Name (Coronation)	154	60			
All Hail the Power of Jesus' Name (Diadem)	155				
Rejoice, Ye Pure in Heart (Marion)	160		130		
Rejoice, Ye Pure in Heart (Vineyard Haven)	161				
All Praise to Thee, for Thou, O King Divine	166				
Canticle of Christ's Obedience	167				
At the Name of Jesus Every Knee Shall Bow	168				
He Is Lord, He Is Lord!	177	173			233
When Morning Gilds the Skies	185		369		
Jesus! the Name High over All	193		199		
Hosanna, Loud Hosanna, the Little Children Sang	278				
All Glory, Laud, and Honor	280				
What Wondrous Love Is This	292				
Christ the Lord Is Risen Today	302	152	193		
And Can It Be that I Should Gain	363	206	280		
Precious Name	536				
Take the Name of Jesus with You	536				
Lord, Whose Love Through Humble Service	581				

Scripture	Hymn Title	UMH	MVPC	CLUW	TFWS	SOZ
	Creator of the Stars of Night	692				
	Rejoice, the Lord Is King (Darwall's 148th)	715				
	Rejoice, the Lord Is King (Gopsal)	716				
	Mothering God, You Gave Me Birth				2050	
	He Is Exalted				2070	
	Jesus, Name above All Names				2071	
	Lord, I Lift Your Name on High				2088	
	Thou Didst Leave Thy Throne				2100	
	Come and See				2127	
	Make Me a Servant				2176	
	The Servant Song				2222	

Luke 22:14–23:56

Scripture	Hymn Title	UMH	MVPC	CLUW	TFWS	SOZ
	To Mock Your Reign, O Dearest Lord	285		184		
	O Love Divine, What Hast Thou Done	287		185		
	Were You There When They Crucified My Lord?	288	137			126
	Ah, Holy Jesus, How Hast Thou Offended	289				
	Go to Dark Gethsemane	290		187		
	He Never Said a Mumbalin' Word	291				101
	They Crucified My Lord	291				
	I Stand Amazed in the Presence	371		93		
	Must Jesus Bear the Cross Alone	424				
	For the Healing of the Nations	428				
	O Master, Let Me Walk with Thee	430		315		
	By Gracious Powers So Wonderfully Sheltered	517				
	Lord, You Give the Great Commission	584				
	For the Bread Which You Have Broken (For the Bread)	614		235		
	For the Bread Which You Have Broken (Beng-Li)	615				
	I Come with Joy to Meet My Lord	617				
	Now the Silence	619				
	Come, Let Us Eat	625				
	O the Depth of Love Divine	627				
	Because Thou Hast Said	635				

Scripture	Hymn Title	UMH	MVPC	CLUW	TFWS	SOZ
	Take Our Bread	640		238		
	Amen, Amen				2072	
	King of Kings				2075	
	Lord, I Lift Your Name on High				2088	
	Thou Didst Leave Thy Throne				2100	
	Hosanna! Hosanna!				2109	
	Why Has God Forsaken Me?				2110	
	Lamb of God				2113	
	Please Enter My Heart, Hosanna				2154	
	Cry of My Heart				2165	
	Now It Is Evening				2187	
	How Long, O Lord				2209	
	Life-giving Bread				2261	
	Broken for Me				2263	
	Time Now to Gather				2265	
	Come, Share the Lord				2269	
	Holy Ground				2272	

April 5, 2007 (Holy Thursday)

Scripture Hymn Title	UMH	MVPC	CLUW	TFWS	SOZ
Exodus 12:1-14					
O God, Our Help in Ages Past	117				
El Shaddai	123	45	77		
Guide Me, O Thou Great Jehovah	127				
He Leadeth Me: O Blessed Thought	128	237			
We Gather Together to Ask the Lord's Blessing	131	361			
Go Down, Moses	448				112
Lead Me, Lord	473				
Wellspring of Wisdom	506				
Jesus, Savior, Lord, Lo, to Thee I Fly	523				
Here, O My Lord, I See Thee	623				
You Satisfy the Hungry Heart	629				
O God Beyond All Praising				2009	
We Bring the Sacrifice of Praise				2031	
Shepherd Me, O God				2058	
God the Sculptor of the Mountains				2060	
Spirit, Spirit of Gentleness				2120	
A Mother Lined a Basket				2189	
Lead On, O Cloud of Presence				2234	
In the Midst of New Dimensions				2238	
Deep in the Shadows of the Past				2246	
He Has Made Me Glad				2270	
Psalm 116:1-2, 12-19					
Thank You, Lord	84				228
What Gift Can We Bring	87				
My Tribute	99				
Praise to the Lord, the Almighty	139	29	68		

Scripture	Hymn Title	UMH	MVPC	CLUW	TFWS	SOZ
	Children of the Heavenly Father	141		335		
	Come, My Way, My Truth, My Life	164				
	More Love to Thee, O Christ	453		318		
	Saranam, Saranam	523		105		
	Jesus, Savior, Lord, Lo, to Thee I Fly	523		105		
	Come, Sinners, to the Gospel Feast (Communion)	616				
	I Will Call upon the Lord				2002	
	We Bring the Sacrifice of Praise				2031	
	Give Thanks				2036	
	I Love You, Lord				2068	
	There Are Some Things I May Not Know				2147	
	O Lord, Hear My Prayer				2200	

1 Corinthians 11:23-26

Scripture	Hymn Title	UMH	MVPC	CLUW	TFWS	SOZ
	O Crucified Redeemer	425				
	Here, O Lord, Your Servants Gather	552		251		
	Lord, You Give the Great Commission	584				
	The Church of Christ, in Every Age	589				
	For the Bread Which You Have Broken	614		235		
	For the Bread Which You Have Broken (Beng-Li)	615				
	Come, Sinners, to the Gospel Feast (Communion)	616				
	I Come With Joy to Meet My Lord	617				
	Let Us Break Bread Together	618	316	236		88
	Bread of the World in Mercy Broken	624		240		
	Eat This Bread, Drink This Cup	628				
	The Bread of Life for All Is Broken	633				
	Because Thou Hast Said	635				
	Una Espiga	637	319			
	Take Our Bread	640		238		
	Mothering God, You Gave Me Birth				2050	
	Now It Is Evening				2187	
	In Remembrance of Me				2254	
	In the Singing				2255	
	Life-giving Bread				2261	
	Broken for Me				2263	

Scripture Hymn Title	UMH	MVPC	CLUW	TFWS	SOZ
Here Is Bread, Here Is Wine				2266	
As We Gather at Your Table				2268	
Come, Share the Lord				2269	

John 13:1-17, 31*b*-35

Scripture Hymn Title	UMH	MVPC	CLUW	TFWS	SOZ
Who Is He in Yonder Stall	190				
O Love, How Deep, How Broad, How High	267				
Jesus' Hands Were Kind Hands	273		176		
O Sacred Head, Now Wounded	286	139			
O Love Divine, What Hast Thou Done	287		185		
Were You There When they Crucified My Lord?	288	137			126
Ah, Holy Jesus, How Hast Thou Offended	289				
Go to Dark Gethsemane	290		187		
What Wondrous Love Is This	292				
Love Divine, All Loves Excelling	384				
The Gift of Love	408		341		
Though I May Speak with Bravest Fire	408		341		
Jesus, Thine All-Victorious Love	422				
Jesu, Jesu, Fill Us with Your Love	432	288	179		
Lord, Speak to Me, That I May Speak	463				
Come Down, O Love Divine	475				
O Thou Who Camest from Above	501		269		
Come, Ye Disconsolate, Where'er Ye Languish	510				
By Gracious Powers So Wonderfully Sheltered	517				
Where Charity and Love Prevail	549				
Lord God, Your Love Has Called Us Here	579				
You Satisfy the Hungry Heart	629				
Draw Us in the Spirit's Tether	632				
Canticle of Love, Response 1	646				
God Is Here	660				
Father, I Adore You				2038	
He Came Down				2085	
We Will Glorify the King of Kings				2087	
We Sang Our Glad Hosannas				2111	

Scripture	Hymn Title	UMH	MVPC	CLUW	TFWS	SOZ
	Make Me a Channel of Your Peace				2171	
	Together We Serve				2175	
	Make Me a Servant				2176	
	Wounded World that Cries for Healing				2177	
	Live in Charity				2179	
	Healer of Our Every Ill				2213	
	The Servant Song				2222	
	They'll Know We Are Christians by Our Love				2223	
	Bind Us Together				2226	
	Let Us Be Bread				2260	
	As We Gather at Your Table				2268	
	Joy in the Morning				2284	

April 6, 2007 (Good Friday)

Scripture Hymn Title	UMH	MVPC	CLUW	TFWS	SOZ
Isaiah 52:13–53:12					
Man of Sorrows! What a Name	165				
Hallelujah! What a Savior	165				
Morning Glory, Starlit Sky	194				
To Mock Your Reign, O Dearest Lord	285		184		
O Sacred Head, Now Wounded	286	139			
Ah, Holy Jesus, How Hast Thou Offended	289				
They Crucified My Lord	291				101
He Never Said a Mumbalin' Word	291				101
What Wondrous Love Is This	292				
Alas! and Did My Savior Bleed	294				8
The Strife Is O'er, the Battle Done	306				
Crown Him with Many Crowns	327	157			
Alas! and Did My Savior Bleed	359	202			8
And Can It Be that I Should Gain	363	206	280		
My Song Is Love Unknown				2083	
Lord, I Lift Your Name on High				2088	
O How He Loves You and Me				2108	
Victim Divine				2259	
Psalm 22					
I'll Praise My Maker While I've Breath	60		123		
Praise, My Soul, the King of Heaven	66				
O Worship the King, All-Glorious Above	73				
All People That on Earth Do Dwell	75		118		
Praise the Lord Who Reigns Above	96		124		
The God of Abraham Praise	116	28			
Be Not Dismayed Whate'er Betide	130	260			
God Will Take Care of You	130	260			

Scripture Hymn Title	UMH	MVPC	CLUW	TFWS	SOZ
Angels from the Realms of Glory	220				
O Sacred Head, Now Wounded	286	139			
Pass Me Not, O Gentle Savior	351		271		
Savior, Like a Shepherd Lead Us	381				
Let Us Plead for Faith Alone	385				
My Faith Looks Up to Thee	452				215
I Will Trust in the Lord	464		292		14
Trust and Obey	467		320		
When We Walk with the Lord	467		320		
Precious Lord, Take My Hand	474		309		179
Come Down, O Love Divine	475				
Remember Me, Remember Me	491		234		235
Out of the Depths I Cry to You	515				
By Gracious Powers So Wonderfully Sheltered	517				
Nobody Knows the Trouble I See	520				170
I Want Jesus to Walk with Me	521		104		95
You Satisfy the Hungry Heart	629				
We Sing of Your Glory				2011	
Glory to God				2033	
Give Thanks				2036	
Jesus, Tempted in the Desert				2105	
Why Has God Forsaken Me?				2110	
Out of the Depths				2136	
Why Stand So Far Away, My God?				2180	
How Long, O Lord				2209	
When We Are Called to Sing Your Praise				2216	
Goodness Is Stronger than Evil				2219	
Taste and See				2267	

Hebrews 10:16-25

	UMH	MVPC	CLUW	TFWS	SOZ
'Tis Finished! The Messiah Dies	282		182		
Blessed Assurance, Jesus Is Mine!	369	65	287		
Come, Thou Fount of Every Blessing	400	42	127		
I Am Thine, O Lord	419	218			
There Is a Place of Quiet Rest	472		324		
Near to the Heart of God	472		324		
Wash, O God, Our Sons and Daughters	605				

Scripture	Hymn Title	UMH	MVPC	CLUW	TFWS	SOZ
	There Is a Fountain Filled with Blood	622				
	This Is the Feast of Victory	638				
	Take Our Bread	640		238		
	Since Jesus Came into My Heart				2140	
	Live in Charity				2179	
	Victim Divine				2259	

John 18:1–19:42

	Man of Sorrows! What a Name	165				
	Hallelujah! What a Savior	165				
	O Sing a Song of Bethlehem	179				
	Who Is He in Yonder Stall	190				
	Morning Glory, Starlit Sky	194				
	I Danced in the Morning	261	128	170		
	Lord of the Dance	261	128	170		
	O Love, How Deep, How Broad, How High	267				
	Woman in the Night	274				
	'Tis Finished! The Messiah Dies	282		182		
	To Mock Your Reign, O Dearest Lord	285		184		
	O Sacred Head, Now Wounded	286	139			
	O Love Divine, What Hast Thou Done	287		185		
	Were You There When They Crucified My Lord?	288	137			126
	Ah, Holy Jesus, How Hast Thou Offended	289				
	Go to Dark Gethsemane	290		187		
	He Never Said a Mumbalin' Word	291				101
	They Crucified My Lord	291				101
	What Wondrous Love Is This	292				
	Alas! and Did My Savior Bleed	294				8
	Sing, My Tongue, the Glorious Battle	296				
	Beneath the Cross of Jesus	297				
	When I Survey the Wondrous Cross (Hamburg)	298	138			
	When I Survey the Wondrous Cross (Rockingham)	299				
	O the Lamb, the Loving Lamb	300				
	They Crucified My Savior	316		189		

Scripture Hymn Title	UMH	MVPC	CLUW	TFWS	SOZ
Hail, Thou Once Despised Jesus	325				
Alas! and Did My Savior Bleed	359	202			8
Rock of Ages, Cleft for Me	361	247			
Jesus, Remember Me	488	249	364		
The Old Rugged Cross	504	142			
O Church of God, United	547		249		
We've a Story to Tell to the Nations	569				
Let All Mortal Flesh Keep Silence	626		150		217
The Bread of Life for All Is Broken	633				
Rejoice, the Lord Is King (Darwall's 148th)	715				
Rejoice, the Lord Is King (Gopsal)	716				
Lo, He Comes with Clouds Descending	718				
Awesome God				2040	
All Hail King Jesus				2069	
My Song Is Love Unknown				2083	
Lord, I Lift Your Name on High				2088	
Thou Didst Leave Thy Throne				2100	
Swiftly Pass the Clouds of Glory				2102	
When Jesus Wept				2106	
O How He Loves You and Me				2108	
Why Has God Forsaken Me				2110	
We Sang Our Glad Hosannas				2111	
Jesus Walked This Lonesome Valley				2112	
Lamb of God				2113	
Living for Jesus				2149	
Here Am I				2178	
Sent Out in Jesus' Name				2184	
Stay with Me				2198	
Stay with Us				2199	
Victim Divine				2259	

April 8, 2007 (Easter Sunday)

Scripture	Hymn Title	UMH	MVPC	CLUW	TFWS	SOZ
Acts 10:34-43						
	Holy God, We Praise Thy Name	79		80		
	God Hath Spoken by the Prophets	108	38			
	O Sing a Song of Bethlehem	179				
	Who Is He in Yonder Stall	190				
	When Jesus Came to Jordan	252	125			
	We Would See Jesus	256		168		
	We Meet You, O Christ	257				
	Lord of the Dance	261	128	170		
	The Strife Is O'er, the Battle Done	306				
	Come, Ye Faithful, Raise the Strain	315				
	Christ Jesus Lay in Death's Strong Bands	319				
	Hail Thee, Festival Day	324				
	For the Healing of the Nations	428				
	This Is My Song	437				
	I Come with Joy to Meet My Lord	617				
	Holy				2019	
	You Alone Are Holy				2077	
	At the Font We Start Our Journey				2114	
	Oh, I Know the Lord's Laid His Hands on Me				2139	
	Come, Be Baptized				2252	
	Water, River, Spirit, Grace				2253	
	He Has Made Me Glad				2270	
Psalm 118:1-2, 14-24						
	Heleluyan, Heleluyan	78	39	354		
	My Tribute	99				
	In Thee Is Gladness	169				
	Alleluia	186		355		

Scripture Hymn Title	UMH	MVPC	CLUW	TFWS	SOZ
Good Christian Friends, Rejoice	224		155		
All Glory, Laud, and Honor	280				
The Day of Resurrection	303		188		
This Is the Day, This Is the Day (This Is the Day)	657				
This Is the Day the Lord Hath Made	658				
Stand Up and Bless the Lord	662		128		
Let Us with a Joyful Mind				2012	
Alleluia (Celtic)				2043	
You Alone Are Holy				2077	
Alleluia (Honduras)				2078	
Thank You, Jesus				2081	
Come, Let Us with Our Lord Arise				2084	

1 Corinthians 15:19-26

Scripture Hymn Title	UMH	MVPC	CLUW	TFWS	SOZ
Hope of the World	178				
Thine Be the Glory, Risen, Conquering Son	308	155	194		
Hail the Day That Sees Him Rise	312	158			
Christ Is Risen, Christ Is Living	313				
Cristo Vive, Fuera El Llanto	313				
Come, Ye Faithful, Raise the Strain	315				
Christ Jesus Lay in Death's Strong Bands	319				
Low in the Grave He Lay	322	147	192		
Up from the Grave He Arose	322	147	192		
And Can It Be that I Should Gain	363	206	280		
Stand Up, Stand Up for Jesus	514				
Christian People, Raise Your Song	636				
Sing with All the Saints in Glory	702		382		
Rejoice, the Lord Is King (Darwall's 148th)	715				
Rejoice, the Lord Is King (Gopsal)	716				
Alleluia (Celtic)				2043	
Lord, I Lift Your Name on High				2088	
Christ Has Risen				2115	
Christ the Lord Is Risen				2116	
Goodness Is Stronger than Evil				2219	

Scripture Hymn Title	UMH	MVPC	CLUW	TFWS	SOZ
John 20:1-18					
O Mary, Don't You Weep, Don't You Mourn	134				153
He Is Lord, He Is Lord!	177	173			233
Alleluia	186		355		
Good Christian Friends, Rejoice	224		155		
Woman in the Night	274				
The First One Ever, Oh, Ever to Know	276				
Christ the Lord Is Risen Today	302	152	193		
The Day of Resurrection	303		188		
Easter People, Raise Your Voices	304				6
The Strife Is O'er, the Battle Done	306				
Christ Is Risen! Shout Hosanna!	307				
Thine Be the Glory, Risen, Conquering Son	308	155	194		
On the Day of Resurrection	309				
I Serve a Risen Savior	310	149			30
He Lives	310	149			30
Now the Green Blade Riseth	311				
Hail the Day That Sees Him Rise	312	158			
Christ Is Risen, Christ Is Living	313				
Cristo Vive, Fuera El Llanto	313				
In the Garden	314	242	296		44
O Sons and Daughters, Let Us Sing	317				
Christ Is Alive! Let Christians Sing	318		190		
Low in the Grave He Lay	322		192		
Crown Him with Many Crowns	327	157			
My Faith Looks Up to Thee	452				215
As Man and Woman We Were Made	642				
Alleluia (Honduras)				2078	
We Sang Our Glad Hosannas				2111	
Christ Has Risen				2115	
Christ the Lord Has Risen				2116	
Walk with Me				2242	
Sing Alleluia to the Lord				2258	

April 15, 2007 (Second Sunday of Easter)

Scripture Hymn Title	UMH	MVPC	CLUW	TFWS	SOZ
Acts 5:27-32					
We Meet You, O Christ	257				
Come, Ye Faithful, Raise the Strain	315				
Low in the Grave He Lay	322	147	192		
Up from the Grave He Arose	322	147	192		
The Head That Once Was Crowned With Thorns	326				
I'm Goin'a Sing When the Spirit Says Sing	333		223		81
When We Walk With the Lord	467		320		
Trust and Obey	467		320		
Stand Up, Stand Up for Jesus	514				
He Is Exalted				2070	
Psalm 150					
When in Our Music God Is Glorified	68		129		
Holy God, We Praise Thy Name	79		80		
Praise God, from Whom All Blessings Flow	94	167	352		
Praise God, from Whom All Blessings Flow	95	21			
Praise the Lord Who Reigns Above	96		124		
Praise to the Lord, the Almighty	139	29	68		
Let All Things Now Living				2008	
Praise Ye the Lord				2010	
Praise the Lord with the Sound of Trumpet				2020	
Halle, Halle, Halleluja				2026	
Sing a New Song to the Lord				2045	
Shout to the Lord				2074	
Alleluia (Honduras)				2078	

Scripture Hymn Title	UMH	MVPC	CLUW	TFWS	SOZ

Revelation 1:4-8

Scripture Hymn Title	UMH	MVPC	CLUW	TFWS	SOZ
Come, Thou Almighty King	61	11			
Glory Be to the Father (Meineke)— Gloria Patri	70	23			
Glory Be to the Father (Greatorex)— Gloria Patri	71				
Maker, in Whom We Live	88				
Ye Watchers and Ye Holy Ones	90				
My Tribute	99				
All Hail the Power of Jesus' Name (Coronation)	154	60			
All Hail the Power of Jesus' Name (Diadem)	155				
Jesus Shall Reign Where'er the Sun	157				
Majesty, Worship His Majesty	176	171	204		
Of the Father's Love Begotten	184	52	66		
When Morning Gilds the Skies	185		369		
Hail to the Lord's Anointed	203	81			
Christ Is Risen, Christ Is Living	313				
Cristo Vive, Fuera El Llanto	313				
Turn Your Eyes upon Jesus	349				
Blessed Assurance, Jesus Is Mine!	369	65	287		
Love Divine, All Loves Excelling	384				
Let All Mortal Flesh Keep Silence	626		150		217
This Is the Feast of Victory	638				
Soon and Very Soon	706		385		198
Lo, He Comes with Clouds Descending	718				
Awesome God				2040	
You Are Worthy				2063	
All Hail King Jesus				2069	
He Is Exalted				2070	
King of Kings				2075	
We Will Glorify the King of Kings				2087	
Bring Forth the Kingdom				2190	
Freedom Is Coming				2192	

Scripture Hymn Title	UMH	MVPC	CLUW	TFWS	SOZ
John 20:19-31					
He Is Lord, He Is Lord!	177	173			233
The First One Ever, Oh, Ever to Know	276				
The Day of Resurrection	303		188		
Easter People, Raise Your Voices	304				6
Christ Is Risen! Shout Hosanna!	307				
Thine Be the Glory, Risen, Conquering Son	308	155	194		
I Serve a Risen Savior	310	149			30
He Lives	310	149			30
Hail the Day That Sees Him Rise	312	158			
O Sons and Daughters, Let Us Sing	317				
Christ Is Alive! Let Christians Sing	318		190		
Christ Jesus Lay in Death's Strong Bands	319				
Holy Spirit, Come, Confirm Us	331		217		
Of All the Spirit's Gifts to Me	336				
Turn Your Eyes upon Jesus	349				
Dona Nobis Pacem	376	360	142		
Love Divine, All Loves Excelling	384				
Forgive Our Sins as We Forgive	390				
Breathe on Me, Breath of God	420				
Holy Spirit, Truth Divine	465				
Send Me, Lord	497		331		
Spirit of God, Descend upon My Heart	500				
Let It Breathe on Me	503				224
When Our Confidence Is Shaken	505				
O Breath of Life, Come Sweeping through Us	543				
Where Charity and Love Prevail	549				
Savior, Again to Thy Dear Name	663	349			
Lo, He Comes with Clouds Descending	718				
Womb of Life				2046	
Christ Has Risen				2115	
Spirit of God				2117	
Where the Spirit of the Lord Is				2119	
Please Enter My Heart, Hosanna				2154	

Scripture	Hymn Title	UMH	MVPC	CLUW	TFWS	SOZ
	God, How Can We Forgive				2169	
	Now It Is Evening				2187	
	We Walk by Faith				2196	
	Without Seeing You				2206	
	Faith Is Patience in the Night				2211	
	Walk with Me				2242	
	In the Singing				2255	
	Here Is Bread, Here Is Wine				2266	

April 22, 2007 (Third Sunday of Easter)

Scripture Hymn Title	UMH	MVPC	CLUW	TFWS	SOZ
Acts 9:1-20					
Depth of Mercy! Can there Be	355		273		
And Can It Be that I Should Gain	363	206	280		
It Is Well with My Soul	377	250	304		20
When Peace, Like a River, Attendeth My Way	377	250	304		20
Amazing Grace! How Sweet the Sound	378	203	94		211
Come, Ye Disconsolate, Where'er Ye Languish	510				
Beams of Heaven as I Go	524				10, 207
Go, Make of All Disciples	571		261		
Whom Shall I Send?	582				
Here I Am, Lord	593	289	263		
I, the Lord of Sea and Sky	593	289	263		
Baptized in Water				2248	
I've Just Come from the Fountain				2250	
We Were Baptized in Christ Jesus				2251	
Psalm 30					
Praise, My Soul, the King of Heaven	66				
Thank You, Lord	84				228
Camina, Pueblo de Dios	305	151			
Walk On, O People of God	305	151			
When Peace, Like a River, Attendeth My Way	377	250	304		20
It Is Well with My Soul	377	250	304		20
Amazing Grace! How Sweet the Sound	378	203	94		211
O Love That Wilt Not Let Me Go	480	255	322		
Come, Ye Disconsolate, Where'er Ye Languish	510				

Scripture Hymn Title	UMH	MVPC	CLUW	TFWS	SOZ
Beams of Heaven as I Go	524				10, 207
Soon and Very Soon	706		385		198
Hymn of Promise	707	338	392		
In the Bulb There Is a Flower	707	338	392		
Come, We That Love the Lord (St. Thomas)	732				
Come, We That Love the Lord (Marching to Zion)	733				3
We're Marching to Zion	733				3
Give Thanks				2036	
Someone Asked the Question				2144	
What Does the Lord Require of You				2174	
O Freedom				2194	
In the Lord I'll Be Ever Thankful				2195	
Joy Comes with the Dawn				2210	
Faith Is Patience in the Night				2211	
I'll Fly Away				2282	
Joy in the Morning				2284	

Revelation 5:11-14

Scripture Hymn Title	UMH	MVPC	CLUW	TFWS	SOZ
O for a Thousand Tongues to Sing	57	1	226		
Mil Voces Para Celebrar	59				
Holy, Holy, Holy! Lord God Almighty	64	4	79		
Holy God, We Praise Thy Name	79		80		
Ye Watchers and Ye Holy Ones	90				
All Hail the Power of Jesus' Name (Coronation)	154	60			
All Hail the Power of Jesus' Name (Diadem)	155				
Hallelujah! What a Savior	165				
Man of Sorrows! What a Name	165				
Ye Servants of God, Your Master Proclaim	181				
O the Lamb, the Loving Lamb	300				
Jaya Ho Jaya Ho	478				
Onward, Christian Soldiers	575	275			
Now the Silence	619				
This Is the Feast of Victory	638				
Fix Me, Jesus	655				122

Scripture Hymn Title	UMH	MVPC	CLUW	TFWS	SOZ
See the Morning Sun Ascending	674				
Lo, He Comes with Clouds Descending	718				
My Lord, What a Morning	719		386		145
Great Is the Lord				2022	
Clap Your Hands				2028	
Awesome God				2040	
Sing a New Song to the Lord				2045	
Lamb of God				2113	
Come and See				2127	
Someone Asked the Question				2144	

John 21:1-19

Scripture Hymn Title	UMH	MVPC	CLUW	TFWS	SOZ
There Is a Name I Love to Hear	170		198		
My Jesus, I Love Thee	172		321		
Christ, Whose Glory Fills the Skies	173		281		
There's a Spirit in the Air	192				
Christ Is Risen! Shout Hosanna!	307				
Lord, You Have Come to the Lakeshore	344	195	90		
Tú Has Venido a La Orilla	344	195	90		
O Jesus, I Have Promised	396	214			
Jesus Calls Us o'er the Tumult	398		96		
Jesu, Jesu, Fill Us with Your Love	432	288	179		
More Love to Thee, O Christ	453		318		
Sweet Hour of Prayer	496	248	330		
Lord, Whose Love Through Humble Service	581				
The Church of Christ, in Every Age	589				
Christ Loves the Church	590				
Rescue the Perishing	591				
Come, Let Us Eat	625				
Christian People, Raise Your Song	636				
Take Our Bread	640		238		
Go Forth for God	670				
The Summons				2130	
Cry of My Heart				2165	

2129
2223
2164
2166

April 29, 2007 (Fourth Sunday of Easter)

Scripture Hymn Title	UMH	MVPC	CLUW	TFWS	SOZ
Acts 9:36-43					
Easter People, Raise Your Voices	304				6
The Strife Is O'er, the Battle Done	306				
Christ Is Risen! Shout Hosanna!	307				
Christ Is Risen, Christ Is Living	313				
Cristo Vive, Fuera el Llanto	313				
Precious Lord, Take My Hand	474		309		179
Send Me, Lord	497		331		
Psalm 23					
He Leadeth Me: O Blessed Thought	128	237			
The Lord's My Shepherd, I'll Not Want	136		115		
Psalm 23 (King James Version)	137				
The King of Love My Shepherd Is	138				
Savior, Like a Shepherd Lead Us	381				
Close to Thee	407				7
Thou My Everlasting Portion	407				7
Precious Lord, Take My Hand	474		309		179
Send Me, Lord	497		331		
O Thou, in Whose Presence My Soul Takes Delight	518				
Give Me the Faith Which Can Remove	650				
Go Now in Peace	665		363		
Lord, Dismiss Us with Thy Blessing	671				
I Was There to Hear Your Borning Cry				2051	
If It Had Not Been for the Lord				2053	
Nothing Can Trouble				2054	
You Are My Hiding Place				2055	
Shepherd Me, O God				2058	

Scripture Hymn Title	UMH	MVPC	CLUW	TFWS	SOZ
Jesus Walked This Lonesome Valley				2112	
Lamb of God				2113	
Come and Find the Quiet Center				2128	
Since Jesus Came into My Heart				2140	
Now It Is Evening				2187	
Without Seeing You				2206	
Lead Me, Guide Me				2214	
You Are Mine				2218	
Goodness Is Stronger than Evil				2219	

Revelation 7:9-17

Scripture Hymn Title	UMH	MVPC	CLUW	TFWS	SOZ
Holy, Holy, Holy! Lord God Almighty	64	4	79		
Maker, in Whom We Live	88				
Ye Watchers and Ye Holy Ones	90				
All Hail the Power of Jesus' Name (Coronation)	154	60			
All Hail the Power of Jesus' Name (Diadem)	155				
Majesty, Worship His Majesty	176	171	204		
Ye Servants of God, Your Master Proclaim	181				
Once in Royal David's City	250		159		
What Wondrous Love Is This	292				
O the Lamb, the Loving Lamb	300				
Hail, Thou Once Despised Jesus	325				
The Head That Once Was Crowned with Thorns	326				
Crown Him with Many Crowns	327	157			
Blessed Assurance, Jesus Is Mine!	369	65	287		
Savior, Like a Shepherd Lead Us	381				
Love Divine, All Loves Excelling	384				
Take My Life, and Let It Be Consecrated	399		312		
My Faith Looks Up to Thee	452				215
Now the Silence	619				
This Is the Feast of Victory	638				
Fill My Cup, Lord	641				
Fix Me, Jesus	655				122
See the Morning Sun Ascending	674				

Scripture	Hymn Title	UMH	MVPC	CLUW	TFWS	SOZ
	Come, Let Us Join Our Friends Above	709		387		
	Glorious Things of Thee Are Spoken	731		256		
	Come, We That Love the Lord (St. Thomas)	732				
	Come, We That Love the Lord (Marching to Zion)	733				3
	Give Thanks				2036	
	Awesome God				2040	
	You Are My Hiding Place				2055	
	Shepherd Me, O God				2058	
	Lamb of God				2113	
	All Who Hunger				2126	
	Bring Forth the Kingdom				2190	
	Come to the Table				2264	
	Holy Ground				2272	
	For All the Saints				2283	

John 10:22-30

Scripture	Hymn Title	UMH	MVPC	CLUW	TFWS	SOZ
	My Tribute	99				
	Thou Hidden Source of Calm Repose	153		346		
	His Name Is Wonderful	174	172	203		
	Jesus, the Very Thought of Thee	175				
	Savior, Like a Shepherd Lead Us	381				
	Close to Thee	407				7
	Thou My Everlasting Portion	407				7
	I Am Thine, O Lord	419	218			
	Near to the Heart of God	472		324		
	O Thou, in Whose Presence My Soul Takes Delight	518				
	You Satisfy the Hungry Heart	629				
	Give Me the Faith Which Can Remove	650				
	Shepherd Me, O God				2058	
	Lamb of God				2113	
	The Summons				2130	
	Would I Have Answered When You Called				2137	

May 6, 2007 (Fifth Sunday of Easter)

Scripture Hymn Title	UMH	MVPC	CLUW	TFWS	SOZ
Acts 11:1-18					
O Let the Son of God Enfold You	347	190	91		
Spirit Song	347	190	91		
Spirit of the Living God, Fall Afresh on Me	393	177	214		226
O Church of God, United	547		249		
In Christ There Is No East or West	548				65
Here, O Lord, Your Servants Gather	552		251		
Help Us Accept Each Other	560		253		
Jesus, United by Thy Grace	561				
Jesus Our Friend and Brother	659				
O Lord, May Church and Home Combine	695				
Spirit of God				2117	
When Cain Killed Abel				2135	
God Made from One Blood				2170	
Make Us One				2224	
Psalm 148					
All Creatures of Our God and King	62	22			
O Lord My God! When I in Awesome Wonder	77	2	61		
How Great Thou Art	77	2	61		
Ye Watchers and Ye Holy Ones	90				
Praise the Lord Who Reigns Above	96		124		
God of the Sparrow God of the Whale	122	37	59		
Sing Praise to God Who Reigns Above	126		60		
Praise to the Lord, the Almighty	139	29	68		
I Sing the Almighty Power of God	152		65		
I Love to Tell the Story	156	56			

Scripture	Hymn Title	UMH	MVPC	CLUW	TFWS	SOZ
	Good Christian Friends, Rejoice	224		155		
	Let All Things Now Living				2008	
	Let Us with a Joyful Mind				2012	
	Come, Rejoice in God				2017	
	Praise the Lord with the Sound of Trumpet				2020	
	What a Mighty God We Serve				2021	
	Great Is the Lord				2022	
	Halle, Halle, Halleluja				2026	
	Clap Your Hands				2028	
	Glory to God				2033	
	Praise, Praise, Praise the Lord				2035	
	Sing a New Song to the Lord				2045	
	We Will Glorify the King of Kings				2087	
	The Trees of the Field				2279	

Revelation 21:1-6

Scripture	Hymn Title	UMH	MVPC	CLUW	TFWS	SOZ
	O God, Our Help in Ages Past	117				
	There's Something About That Name	171	74			
	There's a Spirit in the Air	192				
	O Let the Son of God Enfold You	347	190	91		
	Spirit Song	347	190	91		
	This Is a Day of New Beginnings	383	208	311		
	Love Divine, All Loves Excelling	384				
	O Come and Dwell in Me	388				
	For the Healing of the Nations	428				
	My Faith Looks Up to Thee	452				215
	Come, Ye Disconsolate, Where'er Ye Languish	510				
	Beams of Heaven as I Go	524				10, 207
	We Shall Overcome	533		140		127
	Here, O My Lord, I See Thee	623				
	This Is the Feast of Victory	638				
	Sing with All the Saints in Glory	702		382		
	Soon and Very Soon	706		385		198
	Come, Let Us Join Our Friends Above	709		387		
	I Want to Be Ready	722				151
	O Holy City, Seen of John	726		390		

Scripture Hymn Title	UMH	MVPC	CLUW	TFWS	SOZ
O What Their Joy and Their Glory Must Be	727				
From the Rising of the Sun				2024	
Awesome God				2040	
Open Our Eyes				2086	
We Will Glorify the King of Kings				2087	
All Who Hunger				2126	
You Who Are Thirsty				2132	
Blessed Quietness				2142	
O Freedom				2194	
Joy Comes with the Dawn				2210	
I'll Fly Away				2282	
For All the Saints				2283	
Joy in the Morning				2284	

John 13:31-35

Scripture Hymn Title	UMH	MVPC	CLUW	TFWS	SOZ
Love Divine, All Loves Excelling	384				
The Gift of Love	408	341			
Though I May Speak with Bravest Fire	408	341			
Jesus, Thine All-Victorious Love	422				
Come Down, O Love Divine	475				
O Thou Who Camest From Above	501	269			
Come, Ye Disconsolate, Where'er Ye Languish	510				
Where Charity and Love Prevail	549				
You Satisfy the Hungry Heart	629				
Canticle of Love	646				
He Came Down				2085	
We Will Glorify the King of Kings				2087	
Live in Charity				2179	
Healer of Our Every Ill				2213	
They'll Know We Are Christians by Our Love				2223	
Bind Us Together				2226	
Let Us Be Bread				2260	
Joy in the Morning				2284	

May 13, 2007 (Sixth Sunday of Easter)

Scripture Hymn Title	UMH	MVPC	CLUW	TFWS	SOZ
Acts 16:9-15					
He Leadeth Me: O Blessed Thought	128	237			
In Christ There Is No East or West	548				65
Forward Through the Ages	555				
The Church of Christ, in Every Age	589				
Give Me the Faith Which Can Remove	650				
Open Our Eyes				2086	
Psalm 67					
Holy, Holy, Holy! Lord God Almighty	64	4	79		
We, Thy People, Praise Thee	67		72		
Holy God, We Praise Thy Name	79		80		
Let All the World in Every Corner Sing	93				
God of Grace and God of Glory	577	287			
Lord, Dismiss Us with Thy Blessing	671				
Come, Ye Thankful People, Come	694		241		
Come, Rejoice in God				2017	
Someone Asked the Question				2144	
He Has Made Me Glad				2270	
Revelation 21:10, 22–22:5					
Holy God, We Praise Thy Name	79		80		
Guide Me, O Thou Great Jehovah	127				
There's Something About That Name	171	74			
I Want to Walk as a Child of the Light	206		102		
Turn Your Eyes upon Jesus	349				
Come, Thou Fount of Every Blessing	400	42	127		
For the Healing of the Nations	428				
All Who Love and Serve Your City	433				
Beams of Heaven as I Go	524				10, 207

Scripture	Hymn Title	UMH	MVPC	CLUW	TFWS	SOZ
	Christ Is Made the Sure Foundation	559				
	Soon and Very Soon	706		385		198
	I Want to Be Ready	722				151
	Shall We Gather at the River	723		389		
	Arise, Shine Out, Your Light Has Come	725				
	O Holy City, Seen of John	726		390		
	O What their Joy and their Glory Must Be	727				
	We Will Glorify the King of Kings				2087	
	Come and Find the Quiet Center				2128	
	You Who Are Thirsty				2132	
	Blessed Quietness				2142	
	Shine, Jesus, Shine				2173	
	O Freedom				2194	
	Joy Comes with the Dawn				2210	
	I'll Fly Away				2282	

John 14:23-29

Scripture	Hymn Title	UMH	MVPC	CLUW	TFWS	SOZ
	Of All the Spirit's Gifts to Me	336				
	Come, All of You	350				
	Dona Nobis Pacem	376	360	142		
	There's Within My Heart a Melody	380		289		
	Though I May Speak with Bravest Fire	408		341		
	The Gift of Love	408		341		
	Jesus, Thine All-Victorious Love	422				
	Trust and Obey	467		320		
	When We Walk with the Lord	467		320		
	Come Down, O Love Divine	475				
	Where Charity and Love Prevail	549				
	The Church of Christ, in Every Age	589				
	Blessed Jesus, at Thy Word	596		108		
	Your Love, O God, Has Called Us Here	647				
	Come, Holy Ghost, Our Souls Inspire	651				
	Thou Didst Leave Thy Throne				2100	
	Where the Spirit of the Lord Is				2119	
	Now It Is Evening				2187	
	Healer of Our Every Ill				2213	
	You Are Mine				2218	

May 17, 2007 (Ascension of the Lord)

May also be used Sunday, May 20, 2007.

Scripture Hymn Title	UMH	MVPC	CLUW	TFWS	SOZ
Acts 1:1-11					
All Hail the Power of Jesus' Name (Coronation)	154	60			
All Hail the Power of Jesus' Name (Diadem)	155				
Alleluia, Alleluia! Give Thanks to the Risen Lord	162				
At the Name of Jesus Every Knee Shall Bow	168				
Christ, Whose Glory, Fills the Skies	173		281		
Christ Is the World's Light	188				
Christ the Lord Is Risen Today	302	152	193		
Camina, Pueblo de Dios	305	151			
Thine Be the Glory, Risen, Conquering Son	308	155	194		
Hail the Day That Sees Him Rise	312	158			
Christ Is Risen, Christ Is Living	313				
Cristo Vive, Fuera el Llanto	313				
Come, Ye Faithful, Raise the Strain	315				
Christ Jesus Lay in Death's Strong Bands	319				
Hail Thee, Festival Day	324				
Spirit of Faith, Come Down	332		219		
Come Down, O Love Divine	475				
See How Great a Flame Aspires	541		248		
Like the Murmur of the Dove's Song	544				
Come, Holy Ghost, Our Hearts Inspire	603		218		
He Is Exalted				2070	

Scripture Hymn Title	UMH	MVPC	CLUW	TFWS	SOZ
We Will Glorify the King of Kings				2087	
Lord, I Lift Your Name on High				2088	
At the Font We Start Our Journey				2114	
Christ Has Risen				2115	
Christ the Lord Is Risen				2116	
Spirit of God				2117	
Holy Spirit, Come to Us				2118	
Loving Spirit				2123	
Wonder of Wonders				2247	
I'll Fly Away				2282	

Psalm 47

Scripture Hymn Title	UMH	MVPC	CLUW	TFWS	SOZ
We, Thy People, Praise Thee	67		72		
All People That on Earth Do Dwell	75		118		
Let All the World in Every Corner Sing	93				
Praise the Lord Who Reigns Above	96		124		
Sing Praise to God Who Reigns Above	126		60		
Jesus Shall Reign Where'er the Sun	157				
Majesty, Worship His Majesty	176	171	204		
Christ Is the World's Light	188				
Thine Be the Glory, Risen, Conquering Son	308	155	194		
Hail, Thou Once Despised Jesus	325				
The Head that Once Was Crowned With Thorns	326				
Crown Him with Many Crowns	327	157			
What a Mighty God We Serve				2021	
Clap Your Hands				2028	
Awesome God				2040	
He Is Exalted				2070	
Shout to the Lord				2074	
Lord, I Lift Your Name on High				2088	
We Are Singing/We Are Marching				2235a-b	

Ephesians 1:15-23

Scripture Hymn Title	UMH	MVPC	CLUW	TFWS	SOZ
When in Our Music God Is Glorified	68		129		
Holy God, We Praise Thy Name	79		80		
All Hail the Power of Jesus' Name (Coronation)	154	60			

Scripture Hymn Title	UMH	MVPC	CLUW	TFWS	SOZ
All Hail the Power of Jesus' Name (Diadem)	155				
Jesus Shall Reign Where'er the Sun	157				
His Name Is Wonderful	174	172	203		
Hope of the World	178				
Hail, Thou Once Despised Jesus	325				
The Head that Once Was Crowned With Thorns	326				
Crown Him With Many Crowns	327	157			
My Hope Is Built on Nothing Less	368	261			
Open My Eyes, that I May See	454	184			
Christ Is Made The Sure Foundation	559				
For All the Saints, Who from Their Labors Rest	711	384	388		
Nothing Can Trouble				2054	
You Are Worthy				2063	
Jesus, Name above All Names				2071	
Open Our Eyes				2086	
There Are Some Things I May Not Know				2147	
The Fragrance of Christ				2205	
We Are God's People				2220	
Life-Giving Bread				2261	
Come, Share the Lord				2269	
Glory to God in the Highest				2276	
The Trees of the Field				2279	

Luke 24:44-53

Scripture Hymn Title	UMH	MVPC	CLUW	TFWS	SOZ
Jesus Shall Reign Where'er the Sun	157				
Alleluia, Alleluia! Give Thanks to the Risen Lord	162				
Majesty, Worship His Majesty	176	171	204		
Who Is He in Yonder Stall	190				
Christ the Lord Is Risen Today	302	152	193		
Camina, Pueblo De Dios	305	151			
Christ Is Risen! Shout Hosanna	307				
Hail the Day that Sees Him Rise	312	158			
Christ Is Risen, Christ Is Living	313				
Cristo Vive, Fuera El Llanto	313				

Scripture Hymn Title	UMH	MVPC	CLUW	TFWS	SOZ
Come, Ye Faithful, Raise the Strain	315				
Christ Jesus Lay in Death's Strong Bands	319				
Hail Thee, Festival Day	324				
Hail, Thou Once Despised Jesus	325				
The Head That Once Was Crowned with Thorns	326				
Crown Him With Many Crowns	327	157			
Sent Forth By God's Blessing	664		366		
Rejoice, the Lord Is King (Darwall's 148th)	715				
Rejoice, the Lord Is King (Gopsal)	716				
He Is Exalted				2070	
You Alone Are Holy				2077	
Come, Let Us with Our Lord Arise				2084	
At the Font We Start Our Journey				2114	
Christ Has Risen				2115	
Christ the Lord Is Risen				2116	
Spirit of God				2117	
Sent Out in Jesus' Name				2184	
Go Ye, Go Ye into the World				2239	
The Spirit Sends Us Forth to Serve				2241	
Wonder of Wonders				2247	
I'll Fly Away				2282	

May 20, 2007 (Seventh Sunday of Easter)

Scripture Hymn Title	UMH	MVPC	CLUW	TFWS	SOZ
Acts 16:16-34					
Be Not Dismayed Whate'er Betide	130	260			
God Will Take Care of You	130	260			
Leaning on the Everlasting Arms	133	244	291		53
What a Fellowship, What a Joy Divine	133	244	291		53
And Can It Be that I Should Gain	363	206	280		
He Touched Me	367	209	286		72
Shackled by a Heavy Burden	367	209	286		72
Our Parent, by Whose Name	447				
Stand by Me	512				41
When the Storms of Life Are Raging	512				41
Faith Is Patience in the Night				2211	
Psalm 97					
We, Thy People, Praise Thee	67		72		
Jesus Shall Reign Where'er the Sun	157				
Christ Is the World's Light	188				
O Come, All Ye Faithful	234	106			
Camina, Pueblo de Dios	305	151			
Walk On, O People of God	305	151			
Revelation 22:12-14, 16-17, 20-21					
Christ, Whose Glory, Fills the Skies	173		281		
Of the Father's Love Begotten	184	52	66		
Christ Is the World's Light	188				
O Morning Star, How Fair and Bright	247				
Crown Him With Many Crowns	327	157			
O Let the Son of God Enfold You	347	190	91		
Spirit Song	347	190	91		
Softly and Tenderly Jesus Is Calling	348	193	284		

Scripture	Hymn Title	UMH	MVPC	CLUW	TFWS	SOZ
	Come, All of You	350				
	Blow Ye the Trumpet, Blow	379	309			
	Love Divine, All Loves Excelling	384				
	Deck Thyself, My Soul, with Gladness	612				
	Christian People, Raise Your Song	636				
	Come, Ye Thankful People, Come	694		241		
	Battle Hymn of the Republic	717				24, 213
	Mine Eyes Have Seen the Glory	717				24, 213
	Canticle of Hope, Response	734				
	Honor and Praise				2018	
	The Lily of the Valley				2062	
	All Hail King Jesus				2069	
	O Blessed Spring				2076	
	Star-Child				2095	
	Lord, Listen to Your Children Praying				2193	

John 17:20-26

Scripture	Hymn Title	UMH	MVPC	CLUW	TFWS	SOZ
	The Church's One Foundation	545	269	255		
	O Church of God, United	547		249		
	Here, O Lord, Your Servants Gather	552		251		
	Blest Be the Tie That Binds	557	347			
	Christ Is Made the Sure Foundation	559				
	Help Us Accept Each Other	560		253		
	Father, We Thank You (Albright)	563				
	Father, We Thank You (Rendez À Dieu)	565				
	We Are God's People				2220	

_# 404_

May 27, 2007 (Day of Pentecost)

Scripture Hymn Title	UMH	MVPC	CLUW	TFWS	SOZ
Acts 2:1-21					
Now Thank We All Our God	102				
Surely the Presence of the Lord Is in This Place	328	344	215		
Holy Spirit, Come, Confirm Us	331		217		
Of All the Spirit's Gifts to Me	336				
Spirit of the Living God, Fall Afresh on Me	393	177	214		226
Holy Spirit, Truth Divine	465				
Spirit of God, Descend Upon My Heart	500				
Filled with the Spirit's Power	537				
Wind Who Makes All Winds That Blow	538				
O Spirit of the Living God	539				
I Love Thy Kingdom, Lord	540				
See How Great a Flame Aspires	541		248		
O Breath of Life, Come Sweeping through Us	543				
Like the Murmur of the Dove's Song	544				
The Church's One Foundation	545	269	255		
O Church of God, United	547		249		
Here, O Lord, Your Servants Gather	552		251		
I Am the Church!	558		252		
God of Grace and God of Glory	577	287			
Come, Holy Ghost, Our Souls Inspire	651				
I Will Call upon the Lord				2002	
Holy, Holy				2039	
Mothering God, You Gave Me Birth				2050	
You Alone Are Holy				2077	
Open Our Eyes				2086	
Spirit of God				2117	

87

Scripture Hymn Title	UMH	MVPC	CLUW	TFWS	SOZ
Holy Spirit, Come to Us				2118	
Where the Spirit of the Lord Is				2119	
Spirit, Spirit of Gentleness				2120	
She Comes Sailing on the Wind				2122	
Loving Spirit				2123	
Come, O Holy Spirit, Come				2124	
Come, Holy Spirit				2125	
Eternal Father, Strong to Save				2191	
Gather Us In				2236	
As a Fire Is Meant for Burning				2237	
In the Midst of New Dimensions				2238	
The Spirit Sends Us Forth to Serve				2241	
Deep in the Shadows of the Past				2246	
Come, Share the Lord				2269	
Holy Ground				2272	
For All the Saints				2283	

Psalm 104:24-34, 35*b*

Scripture Hymn Title	UMH	MVPC	CLUW	TFWS	SOZ
All Creatures of Our God and King	62	22			
Holy, Holy, Holy! Lord God Almighty	64	4	79		
O Worship the King, All-Glorious Above	73				
Immortal, Invisible, God Only Wise	103		74		
God of the Sparrow God of the Whale	122	37	59		
This Is My Father's World	144	47	62		
Many and Great, O God, Are Thy Things	148	50	71		
Breathe on Me, Breath of God	420				
Wind Who Makes All Winds That Blow	538				
Bless the Lord				2013	
What a Mighty God We Serve				2021	
I Sing Praises to Your Name				2037	
Praise Our God Above				2061	

Romans 8:14-17

Scripture Hymn Title	UMH	MVPC	CLUW	TFWS	SOZ
Daw-Kee, Aim Daw-Tsi-Taw	330				
I'm Goin'a Sing When the Spirit Says Sing	333		223		81
How Can We Sinners Know	372		288		
Spirit of the Living God, Fall Afresh on Me	393	177	214		226

Scripture Hymn Title	UMH	MVPC	CLUW	TFWS	SOZ
Every Time I Feel the Spirit	404		213		121
Thou Hidden Love of God	414				
Spirit of God, Descend upon My Heart	500				
O Thou Who Camest from Above	501		269		
In Christ There Is No East or West	548				65
Gather Us In				2236	
Baptized in Water				2248	

John 14:8-17, 25-27

Scripture Hymn Title	UMH	MVPC	CLUW	TFWS	SOZ
Source and Sovereign, Rock and Cloud	113				
Christ Is the World's Light	188				
Daw-Kee, Aim Daw-Tsi-Taw	330				
Of All the Spirit's Gifts to Me	336				
Because He Lives	364	154	285		
Dona Nobis Pacem	376	360	142		
Love Divine, All Loves Excelling	384				
Seek Ye First the Kingdom of God	405	201	136		
Canticle of Prayer	406				
Jesus, Thine All-Victorious Love	422				
Filled with the Spirit's Power	537				
O Spirit of the Living God	539				
See How Great a Flame Aspires	541		248		
Like the Murmur of the Dove's Song	544				
Christ Is Made the Sure Foundation	559				
Blessed Jesus, at Thy Word	596		108		
Come, Holy Ghost, Our Souls Inspire	651				
Go Now in Peace	665		363		
Nothing Can Trouble				2054	
He Came Down				2085	
Spirit of God				2117	
Where the Spirit of the Lord Is				2119	
Loving Spirit				2123	
Now It Is Evening				2187	
Healer of Our Every Ill				2213	
You Are Mine				2218	
In the Singing				2255	
Here Is Bread, Here Is Wine				2266	

June 3, 2007 (Trinity Sunday; First Sunday after Pentecost)

Scripture Hymn Title	UMH	MVPC	CLUW	TFWS	SOZ
Proverbs 8:1-4, 22-31					
All Creatures of Our God and King	62	22			
Maker, in Whom We Live	88				
For the Beauty of the Earth	92	8			
God, Whose Love Is Reigning o'er Us	100		73		
Canticle of Wisdom	112				
Source and Sovereign, Rock and Cloud	113				
God Created Heaven and Earth	151				
I Sing the Almighty Power of God	152		65		
Let All Things Now Living				2008	
Womb of Life				2046	
Bring Many Names				2047	
Mothering God, You Gave Me Birth				2050	
Eternal Father, Strong to Save				2191	
Psalm 8					
All Creatures of Our God and King	62	22			
Praise, My Soul, the King of Heaven	66				
O Lord My God! When I in Awesome Wonder	77	2	61		
How Great Thou Art	77	2	61		
Joyful, Joyful, We Adore Thee	89	5	75		
For the Beauty of the Earth	92	8			
For the Fruits of This Creation	97				
God, Whose Love Is Reigning o'er Us	100		73		
O God, Our Help in Ages Past	117				
O God in Heaven, Grant to Thy Children	119		227		
Children of the Heavenly Father	141		335		
Many and Great, O God, Are Thy Things	148	50	71		

Scripture	Hymn Title	UMH	MVPC	CLUW	TFWS	SOZ
	God Created Heaven and Earth	151				
	I Sing the Almighty Power of God	152		65		
	Creator of the Earth and Skies	450				
	Prayer Is the Soul's Sincere Desire	492				
	O God Beyond All Praising				2009	
	Great Is the Lord				2022	
	How Majestic Is Your Name				2023	
	From the Rising of the Sun				2024	
	Awesome God				2040	
	Amen, We Praise Your Name, O God				2067	
	Glory to God in the Highest				2276	

Romans 5:1-5

Scripture	Hymn Title	UMH	MVPC	CLUW	TFWS	SOZ
	We Believe in One True God	85				
	Hail, Thou Once Despised Jesus	325				
	Marvelous Grace of Our Loving Lord	365				
	Grace Greater than Our Sin	365				
	Let Us Plead for Faith Alone	385				
	Come, Thou Fount of Every Blessing	400	42	127		
	Jesus, Thine All-Victorious Love	422				
	O Master, Let Me Walk with Thee	430		315		
	Come Down, O Love Divine	475				
	O Love that Wilt Not Let Me Go	480	255	322		
	When Our Confidence Is Shaken	505				
	O Thou Who This Mysterious Bread	613				
	O Perfect Love, All Human Thought Transcending	645				
	Come, Holy Ghost, Our Souls Inspire	651				
	Rejoice, the Lord Is King (Darwall's 148th)	715				
	Rejoice, the Lord Is King (Gopsal)	716				
	We Walk by Faith				2196	
	In the Singing				2255	
	Sing Alleluia to the Lord				2258	
	As We Gather at Your Table				2268	

John 16:12-15

Scripture	Hymn Title	UMH	MVPC	CLUW	TFWS	SOZ
	Come, Thou Almighty King	61	11			
	O God in Heaven, Grant to Thy Children	119		227		

Scripture Hymn Title	UMH	MVPC	CLUW	TFWS	SOZ
Spirit of the Living God, Fall Afresh on Me	393	177	214		226
Creator of the Earth and Skies	450				
Holy Spirit, Truth Divine	465				
Come Down, O Love Divine	475				
Kum Ba Yah, My Lord	494		332		139
O Spirit of the Living God	539				
O Thou Who This Mysterious Bread	613				
Come, Holy Ghost, Our Souls Inspire	651				

June 10, 2007 (Second Sunday after Pentecost)

Scripture Hymn Title	UMH	MVPC	CLUW	TFWS	SOZ
1 Kings 17:8-24					
Children of the Heavenly Father	141		335		
I Will Trust in the Lord	464		292		14
Psalm 146					
O For a Thousand Tongues to Sing	57	1	226		
Mil Voces Para Celebrar	59	1			
I'll Praise My Maker While I've Breath	60		123		
All My Hope Is Firmly Grounded	132				
Hope of the World	178				
Tell Out, My Soul, the Greatness of the Lord	200				
Lord, I Lift Your Name on High				2088	
Someone Asked the Question				2144	
In the Singing				2255	
Galatians 1:11-24					
Holy Spirit, Come, Confirm Us	331		217		
Filled with the Spirit's Power	537				
Whom Shall I Send?	582				
Luke 7:11-17					
O Mary, Don't You Weep, Don't You Mourn	134				153
He Is Lord, He Is Lord	177	173			233
Easter People, Raise Your Voices	304				6
Come, Ye Disconsolate, Where'er Ye Languish	510				
Abide With Me; Fast Falls the Eventide	700				

June 17, 2007 (Third Sunday after Pentecost)

Scripture Hymn Title	UMH	MVPC	CLUW	TFWS	SOZ
1 Kings 21:1-21*a*					
Righteous and Just Is the Word of Our Lord	107				
La Palabra Del Señor Es Recta	107				
God Hath Spoken by the Prophets	108	38			
O God of Every Nation	435				
What Does the Lord Require	441				
Creator of the Earth and Skies	450				
God of Grace and God of Glory	577	287			
Psalm 5:1-8					
La Palabra Del Señor Es Recta	107				
Righteous and Just Is the Word of Our Lord	107				
Praise to the Lord, the Almighty	139	29	68		
Dear Lord, Lead Me Day by Day	411		100		
O God of Every Nation	435				
Lead Me, Lord	473				
My Prayer Rises to Heaven	498				
Lord, Listen to Your Children				2207	
Lead Me, Guide Me				2214	
Cares Chorus				2215	
Walk with Me				2242	
Galatians 2:15-21					
Alleluia, Alleluia! Give Thanks to the Risen Lord	162				
Alas! and Did My Savior Bleed	294				8
I Sought the Lord, and Afterward I Knew	341				
Pass Me Not, O Gentle Savior	351		271		

Scripture	Hymn Title	UMH	MVPC	CLUW	TFWS	SOZ
	Pues Si Vivimos	356	337	310		
	Let Us Plead for Faith Alone	385				
	Thou Hidden Love of God	414				
	What Does the Lord Require	441				
	Now Let Us from This Table Rise	634				
	O How He Loves You and Me				2108	
	Grace Alone				2162	
	Make Me a Channel of Your Peace				2171	
	We Walk by Faith				2196	
	Faith Is Patience in the Night				2211	

Luke 7:36–8:3

Scripture	Hymn Title	UMH	MVPC	CLUW	TFWS	SOZ
	God Hath Spoken by the Prophets	108	38			
	Heal Us, Emmanuel, Hear Our Prayer	266		328		
	Woman in the Night	274				
	Come, Sinners, to the Gospel Feast (Invitation)	339		88		
	Come, Ye Sinners, Poor and Needy	340				
	Shackled by a Heavy Burden	367	209	286		72
	He Touched Me	367	209	286		72
	Forgive Our Sins as We Forgive	390				
	Something Beautiful, Something Good	394		303		
	What Does the Lord Require	441				
	Come, Sinners, to the Gospel Feast (Communion)	616				
	Go Now in Peace	665		363		
	Two Fishermen				2101	
	I Have Decided to Follow Jesus				2129	
	The Summons				2130	
	I'm So Glad Jesus Lifted Me				2151	
	God, How Can We Forgive				2169	

June 24, 2007 (Fourth Sunday after Pentecost)

Scripture Hymn Title	UMH	MVPC	CLUW	TFWS	SOZ
1 Kings 19:1-15a					
How Like a Gentle Spirit	115		216		
God of the Sparrow God of the Whale	122	37	59		
Guide Me, O Thou Great Jehovah	127				
Give to the Winds Thy Fears	129		282		
Be Not Dismayed Whate'er Betide	130				
Lord, Who Throughout These Forty Days	269		181		
Dear Lord and Father of Mankind	358				
There Is a Balm in Gilead	375	262	98		123
Jaya Ho Jaya Ho	478				
God of Love and God of Power	578				
O Food to Pilgrims Given	631				
Fill My Cup, Lord	641				
God the Spirit, Guide and Guardian	648				
Spirit, Spirit of Gentleness				2120	
Healer of Our Every Ill				2213	
Psalm 42					
Creating God, Your Fingers Trace	109				
Happy the Home When God Is there	445				
My Prayer Rises to Heaven	498				
Be Still, My Soul	534		307		
God of Love and God of Power	578				
As the Deer				2025	
The Lone, Wild Bird				2052	
All I Need Is You				2080	
Cry of My Heart				2165	
More Like You				2167	

Scripture Hymn Title	UMH	MVPC	CLUW	TFWS	SOZ
Galatians 3:23-29					
For the Healing of the Nations	428				
In Christ There Is No East or West	548				65
Where Charity and Love Prevail	549				
Christ, From Whom All Blessings Flow	550		250		
I Am the Church!	558		252		
You Have Put On Christ	609				
One Bread, One Body	620	324	237		
Who Is My Mother, Who Is My Brother				2225	
Luke 8:26-39					
Jesus! the Name High over All	193		199		
Heal Me, Hands of Jesus	262				
When Jesus the Healer Passed Through Galilee	263		171		
Silence, Frenzied, Unclean Spirit	264				
Christ Is Risen! Shout Hosanna	307				
Freely, Freely	389		258		
God Forgave My Sin in Jesus' Name	389		258		
This Little Light of Mine	585		338		132
Sent Forth By God's Blessing	664		366		
Eternal Father, Strong to Save				2191	

July 1, 2007 (Fifth Sunday after Pentecost)

Scripture Hymn Title	UMH	MVPC	CLUW	TFWS	SOZ
2 Kings 2:1-2, 6-14					
O Lord My God! When I in Awesome Wonder	77	2	61		
How Great Thou Art	77	2	61		
Source and Sovereign, Rock and Cloud	113				
Children of the Heavenly Father	141		335		
Hail to the Lord's Anointed	203	81			
Angels from the Realms of Glory	220				
Daw-Kee, Aim Daw-Tsi-Taw	330				
Spirit of the Living God, Fall Afresh on Me	393	177	214		226
Spirit of God, Descend Upon My Heart	500				
Wind Who Makes All Winds that Blow	538				
Come, Holy Ghost, Our Hearts Inspire	603		218		
Come, Holy Ghost, Our Souls Inspire	651				
Canticle of Remembrance	652				
Swing Low, Sweet Chariot	703		384		104
Steal Away to Jesus	704		378		134
Arise, Shine				2005	
Honor and Praise				2018	
Awesome God				2040	
All Hail King Jesus				2069	
He Is Exalted				2070	
Spirit of God				2117	
Come, O Holy Spirit, Come				2124	
Lord, Listen to Your Children				2207	
Psalm 77:1-2, 11-20					
Children of the Heavenly Father	141		335		
God Created Heaven and Earth	151				

Scripture Hymn Title	UMH	MVPC	CLUW	TFWS	SOZ
I Sing the Almighty Power of God	152		65		
Abide with Me; Fast Falls the Eventide	700				
How Long, O Lord				2209	
When We Are Called to Sing Your Praise				2216	
By the Babylonian Rivers				2217	

Galatians 5:1, 13-25

Scripture Hymn Title	UMH	MVPC	CLUW	TFWS	SOZ
For the Fruits of This Creation	97				
A Mighty Fortress Is Our God	110	25			
Of All the Spirit's Gifts to Me	336				
Love Divine, All Loves Excelling	384				
Spirit of the Living God, Fall Afresh on Me	393	177	214		226
For the Healing of the Nations	428				
O Master, Let Me Walk with Thee	430		315		
Spirit of God, Descend upon My Heart	500				
Like the Murmur of the Dove's Song	544				
Where Charity and Love Prevail	549				
Lord God, Your Love Has Called Us Here	579				
Now the Silence	619				
Come, Holy Ghost, Our Souls Inspire	651				
He Came Down				2085	
Spirit of God				2117	
Spirit, Spirit of Gentleness				2120	
Loving Spirit				2123	
When Cain Killed Abel				2135	
Make Me a Channel of Your Peace				2171	
Make Me a Servant				2176	
Live in Charity				2179	
O Freedom				2194	
Lord of All Hopefulness				2197	
Healer of Our Every Ill				2213	
The Servant Song				2222	
They'll Know We Are Christians by Our Love				2223	
In Remembrance of Me				2254	

Scripture Hymn Title	UMH	MVPC	CLUW	TFWS	SOZ
Luke 9:51-62					
Lift High the Cross	159	164	174		
Ye Servants of God, Your Master Proclaim	181				
I Want to Walk as a Child of the Light	206		102		
I Can Hear My Savior Calling	338				42
Where He Leads Me	338				42
O Jesus, I Have Promised	396	214			
Jesus Calls Us O'er the Tumult	398		96		
Lord, I Want to Be a Christian	402	215			76
Close to Thee	407				7
Thou My Everlasting Portion	407				
Take Up Thy Cross, the Savior Said	415		145		
Am I a Soldier of the Cross	511				
My Song Is Love Unknown				2083	
Thou Didst Leave Thy Throne				2100	
Two Fishermen				2101	
Come and See				2127	
The Summons				2130	
Would I Have Answered When You Called				2137	
Cry of My Heart				2165	

July 8, 2007 (Sixth Sunday after Pentecost)

Scripture Hymn Title	UMH	MVPC	CLUW	TFWS	SOZ
2 Kings 5:1-14					
Praise, My Soul, the King of Heaven	66				
We, Thy People, Praise Thee	67		72		
The God of Abraham Praise	116	28			
Praise to the Lord, the Almighty	139	29	68		
O Christ, the Healer, We Have Come	265				
Heal Us, Emmanuel, Hear Our Prayer	266		328		
Come, Ye Sinners, Poor and Needy	340				
Spirit of the Living God, Fall Afresh on Me	393	177	214		226
Wash, O God, Our Sons and Daughters	605				
Honor and Praise				2018	
Gather Us In				2236	
I've Just Come from the Fountain				2250	
Water, River, Spirit, Grace				2253	
Psalm 30					
Praise, My Soul, the King of Heaven	66				
Thank You, Lord	84				228
Camina, Pueblo De Dios	305	151			
Walk On, O People of God	305	151			
It Is Well with My Soul	377	250	304		20
When Peace, Like a River, Attendeth My Way	377	250	304		20
Amazing Grace! How Sweet the Sound	378	203	94		211
O Love that Wilt Not Let Me Go	480	255	322		
Come, Ye Disconsolate, Where'er Ye Languish	510				
Beams of Heaven as I Go	524				10, 207
Soon and Very Soon	706		385		198

101

Scripture Hymn Title	UMH	MVPC	CLUW	TFWS	SOZ
Hymn of Promise	707	338	392		
In the Bulb There Is a Flower	707	338	392		
Come, We That Love the Lord (St. Thomas)	732				
Come, We That Love the Lord (Marching to Zion)	733				3
We're Marching to Zion	733				3
Give Thanks				2036	
Someone Asked the Question				2144	
What Does the Lord Require of You				2174	
O Freedom				2194	
In the Lord I'll Be Ever Thankful				2195	
Joy Comes with the Dawn				2210	
Faith Is Patience in the Night				2211	
I'll Fly Away				2282	
Joy in the Morning				2284	

Galatians 6:1-16

Scripture Hymn Title	UMH	MVPC	CLUW	TFWS	SOZ
For the Fruits of This Creation	97				
Lift High the Cross	159	164	174		
Ask Ye What Great Thing I Know	163				
There's a Spirit in the Air	192				
In the Cross of Christ I Glory	295				
Beneath the Cross of Jesus	297				
When I Survey the Wondrous Cross (Hamburg)	298	138			
When I Survey the Wondrous Cross (Rockingham)	299				
The Head that Once Was Crowned With Thorns	326				
Take Time to Be Holy	395				
The Old Rugged Cross	504	142			
On a Hill Far Away Stood An Old Rugged Cross	504	142			
And Are We Yet Alive	553				
Blest Be the Tie that Binds	557	347			
Jesus, United By Thy Grace	561				
Jesus, Lord, We Look to Thee	562				

Scripture Hymn Title	UMH	MVPC	CLUW	TFWS	SOZ
Lord, Whose Love Through Humble Service	581				
We Know that Christ Is Raised	610		231		
I Was There to Hear Your Borning Cry				2051	
Healer of Our Every Ill				2213	
The Servant Song				2222	
Make Us One				2224	
Who Is My Mother, Who Is My Brother				2225	
Let Us Be Bread				2260	
Time Now to Gather				2265	
Come, Share the Lord				2269	

Luke 10:1-11, 16-20

Scripture Hymn Title	UMH	MVPC	CLUW	TFWS	SOZ
For the Fruits of This Creation	97				
When Jesus the Healer Passed Through Galilee	263		171		
Hail, Thou Once Despised Jesus	325				
Dear Lord, for All in Pain	458				
We've a Story to Tell to the Nations	569				
O Zion, Haste	573				
Lord, You Give the Great Commission	584				
The Church of Christ, in Every Age	589				
Here I Am, Lord	593	289	263		
I, the Lord of Sea and Sky	593	289	263		
Come, Let Us Eat	625				
How Shall They Hear the Word of God	649				
Make Me a Channel of Your Peace				2171	
For One Great Peace				2185	
Song of Hope				2186	
Healer of Our Every Ill				2213	
Gather Us In				2236	
In Remembrance of Me				2254	
Let Us Be Bread				2260	
Come, Share the Lord				2269	

July 15, 2007 (Seventh Sunday after Pentecost)

Scripture Hymn Title	UMH	MVPC	CLUW	TFWS	SOZ
Amos 7:7-17					
God Hath Spoken by the Prophets	108	38			
For the Healing of the Nations	428				
Rejoice in God's Saints	708				
Mine Eyes Have Seen the Glory	717				
Battle Hymn of the Republic	717				24, 213
O Day of God, Draw Nigh	730				
God Weeps				2048	
Psalm 82					
Sing Praise to God Who Reigns Above	126		60		
We Gather Together to Ask the Lord's Blessing	131	361			
If Thou But Suffer God to Guide Thee	142				
God Created Heaven and Earth	151				
For the Healing of the Nations	428				
This Is My Song	437				
What Does the Lord Require	441				
God of Grace and God of Glory	577	287			
Mine Eyes Have Seen the Glory	717				
Battle Hymn of the Republic	717				24, 213
Give Thanks				2036	
Bring Many Names				2047	
God Weeps				2048	
What Does the Lord Require of You				2174	
Colossians 1:1-14					
There's a Spirit in the Air	192				
Pues Si Vivimos	356	337	310		
O Jesus, I Have Promised	396	214			

Scripture Hymn Title	UMH	MVPC	CLUW	TFWS	SOZ
Dear Lord, Lead Me Day by Day	411		100		
See How Great a Flame Aspires	541		248		
Forward Through the Ages	555				
God of Grace and God of Glory	577	287			
Lord, Dismiss Us with Thy Blessing	671				
Rejoice in God's Saints	708				
I Sing a Song of the Saints of God	712				
Come, We That Love the Lord (St. Thomas)	732				
Come, We That Love the Lord (Marching to Zion)	733				3
We're Marching to Zion	733				3
Give Thanks				2036	
Mothering God, You Gave Me Birth				2050	
We Need a Faith				2181	
In the Lord I'll Be Ever Thankful				2195	
May You Run and Not Be Weary				2281	

Luke 10:25-37

Scripture Hymn Title	UMH	MVPC	CLUW	TFWS	SOZ
God of the Sparrow God of the Whale	122	37	59		
El Shaddai	123	45	77		
There's a Spirit in the Air	192				
Love Came Down at Christmas	242				
Pues Si Vivimos	356	337	310		
Lord, I Want to Be a Christian	402	215			76
O for a Heart to Praise My God	417				
Where Cross the Crowded Ways of Life	427	296			
Jesu, Jesu, Fill Us with Your Love	432	288	179		
More Love to Thee, O Christ	453		318		
My God, I Love Thee	470				
Come Down, O Love Divine	475				
Spirit of God, Descend Upon My Heart	500				
Where Charity and Love Prevail	549				
Rise Up, O Men of God	576				
Canticle of Love	646				
Your Love, O God, Has Called Us Here	647				
The Summons				2130	

Scripture	Hymn Title	UMH	MVPC	CLUW	TFWS	SOZ
	Sunday's Palms Are Wednesday's Ashes				2138	
	To Know You More				2161	
	More Like You				2167	
	Love the Lord Your God				2168	
	Make Me a Channel of Your Peace				2171	
	Live in Charity				2179	
	Now It Is Evening				2187	
	Healer of Our Every Ill				2213	
	In Remembrance of Me				2254	

July 22, 2007 (Eighth Sunday after Pentecost)

Scripture Hymn Title	UMH	MVPC	CLUW	TFWS	SOZ
Amos 8:1-12					
Of the Father's Love Begotten	184	52	66		
All Who Love and Serve Your City	433				
What Does the Lord Require	441				
Jesus, Lord, We Look to Thee	562				
When the Church of Jesus Shuts Its Outer Door	592				
My Lord, What a Morning	719		386		145
O Holy City, Seen of John	726		390		
God Weeps				2048	
Why Stand So Far Away, My God?				2180	
Psalm 52					
Thank You, Lord	84				228
Why Stand So Far Away, My God?				2180	
How Long, O Lord				2209	
Colossians 1:15-28					
Immortal, Invisible, God Only Wise	103		74		
A Mighty Fortress Is Our God	110	25			
Alleluia, Alleluia! Give Thanks to the Risen Lord	162				
Hope of the World	178				
Of the Father's Love Begotten	184	52	66		
Rise, Shine, You People	187				
Jesus! the Name High over All	193		199		
Jesus, Keep Me Near the Cross	301				19
Camina, Pueblo De Dios	305	151			
Walk On, O People of God	305				
The Strife Is O'er, the Battle Done	306				
Hail, Thou Once Despised Jesus	325				

Scripture Hymn Title	UMH	MVPC	CLUW	TFWS	SOZ
I Heard an Old, Old Story	370		92		
Victory in Jesus	370		92		
When Peace, Like a River, Attendeth My Way	377	250	304		20
It Is Well with My Soul	377	250	304		20
More Love to Thee, O Christ	453		318		
Am I a Soldier of the Cross	511				
Lift Every Voice and Sing	519				32
Christ Is Made the Sure Foundation	559				
Jesus, Lord, We Look to Thee	562				
The Church of Christ, in Every Age	589				
O Splendor of God's Glory Bright	679				
Praise the Source of Faith and Learning				2004	
My Life Is in You, Lord				2032	
Thou Art Worthy				2041	
Jesus, Name above All Names				2071	
O Holy Spirit, Root of Life				2121	
Sanctuary				2164	
Christ Beside Me				2166	
Shine, Jesus, Shine				2173	
Make Me a Servant				2176	
We Are God's People				2220	
As a Fire Is Meant for Burning				2237	
Life-giving Bread				2261	
Holy Ground				2272	

Luke 10:38-42

Scripture Hymn Title	UMH	MVPC	CLUW	TFWS	SOZ
Woman in the Night	274				
Turn Your Eyes upon Jesus	349				
Dear Lord and Father of Mankind	358				
O Jesus, I Have Promised	396	214			
Take My Life, and Let It Be Consecrated	399		312		
All Who Love and Serve Your City	433				
Our Parent, by Whose Name	447				
Be Thou My Vision	451	240			
Jesus, Priceless Treasure	532				
Jesus, Lord, We Look to Thee	562				
Come and Find the Quiet Center				2128	
Come Away with Me				2202	

July 29, 2007 (Ninth Sunday after Pentecost)

Scripture Hymn Title	UMH	MVPC	CLUW	TFWS	SOZ
Hosea 1:2-10					
God Hath Spoken by the Prophets	108	38			
Rise Up, O Men of God	576				
Whom Shall I Send?	582				
God, How Can We Forgive				2169	
Why Stand So Far Away, My God?				2180	
How Long, O Lord				2209	
By the Babylonian Rivers				2217	
Lead On, O Cloud of Presence				2234	
Psalm 85					
O God, Our Help in Ages Past	117				
O God in Heaven, Grant to Thy Children	119		227		
Send Your Word	195		113		
O Come, O Come, Emmanuel	211	80			
Lift Up Your Heads, Ye Mighty Gates	213				
Love Divine, All Loves Excelling	384				
Forgive Our Sins as We Forgive	390				
God of Grace and God of Glory	577	287			
Savior, Again to Thy Dear Name	663	349			
Why Stand So Far Away, My God?				2180	
How Long, O Lord				2209	
By the Babylonian Rivers				2217	
Lead On, O Cloud of Presence				2234	
Colossians 2:6-19					
Now Thank We All Our God	102				
Alleluia, Alleluia! Give Thanks to the Risen Lord	162				
Rise, Shine, You People	187				

Scripture Hymn Title	UMH	MVPC	CLUW	TFWS	SOZ
Camina, Pueblo De Dios	305	151			
Walk On, O People of God	305	151			
The Strife Is O'er, the Battle Done	306				
Hail Thee, Festival Day	324				
Crown Him With Many Crowns	327	157			
When Peace, Like a River, Attendeth My Way	377	250	304		20
It Is Well with My Soul	377	250	304		20
Forgive Our Sins as We Forgive	390				
Come, Thou Fount of Every Blessing	400	42	127		
Close to Thee	407				7
Thou My Everlasting Portion	407				7
A Charge to Keep I Have	413				
Jesus, Thine All-Victorious Love	422				
O Master, Let Me Walk with Thee	430		315		
I Want Jesus to Walk with Me	521		104		95
The Church's One Foundation	545	269	255		
The Church's One Foundation	546				
Christ Is Made the Sure Foundation	559				
Give Thanks				2036	
We Are God's People				2220	
Baptized in Water				2248	
God Claims You				2249	
We Were Baptized in Christ Jesus				2251	
Life-giving Bread				2261	
As We Gather at Your Table				2268	
Come, Share the Lord				2269	

Luke 11:1-13

Scripture Hymn Title	UMH	MVPC	CLUW	TFWS	SOZ
Be Not Dismayed Whate'er Betide	130	260			
God Will Take Care of You	130	260			
The Lord's Prayer (West Indian)	271				
Our Father, Which Art in Heaven	271				
Forgive Our Sins as We Forgive	390				
Every Time I Feel the Spirit	404		213		121
Seek Ye First the Kingdom of God	405	201	136		
Canticle of Prayer	406				
Let There Be Light	440				

Scripture	Hymn Title	UMH	MVPC	CLUW	TFWS	SOZ
	Prayer Is the Soul's Sincere Desire	492				
	Sweet Hour of Prayer	496	248	330		
	Where Charity and Love Prevail	549				
	For the Bread Which You Have Broken (For the	614		235		
	For the Bread Which You Have Broken (Beng-Li)	615				
	Jesus, Joy of Our Desiring	644		344		
	Loving Spirit				2123	
	Sunday's Palms Are Wednesday's Ashes				2138	
	God, How Can We Forgive				2169	
	Make Me a Channel of Your Peace				2171	
	Now It Is Evening				2187	
	Lord, Listen to Your Children Praying				2193	
	We Walk by Faith				2196	
	Come Away with Me				2202	
	The Fragrance of Christ				2205	
	Lord, Listen to Your Children				2207	
	Let Us Offer to the Father				2262	
	As We Gather at Your Table				2268	
	Come, Share the Lord				2269	
	The Lord's Prayer				2278	

August 5, 2007 (Tenth Sunday after Pentecost)

Scripture Hymn Title	UMH	MVPC	CLUW	TFWS	SOZ
Hosea 11:1-11					
Now Thank We All Our God	102				
There's a Wideness in God's Mercy	121				
Sing Praise to God Who Reigns Above	126		60		
Guide Me, O Thou Great Jehovah	127				
Be Not Dismayed Whate'er Betide	130	260			
God Will Take Care of You	130	260			
Great Is Thy Faithfulness	140	30	81		
If Thou But Suffer God to Guide Thee	142				
O God Who Shaped Creation	443				
O Love That Wilt Not Let Me Go	480	255	322		
We Sing to You, O God				2001	
Let All Things Now Living				2008	
Bring Many Names				2047	
Why Stand So Far Away, My God?				2180	
How Long, O Lord				2209	
Lead On, O Cloud of Presence				2234	
Psalm 107:1-9, 43					
Now Thank We All Our God	102				
Guide Me, O Thou Great Jehovah	127				
Be Not Dismayed Whate'er Betide	130				
God Will Take Care of You	130	260			
Great Is Thy Faithfulness	140	30	81		
If Thou But Suffer God to Guide Thee	142				
Come, All of You	350				
Wellspring of Wisdom	506				
Jesus, Joy of Our Desiring	644		344		
Wake, Awake, for Night Is Flying	720				

Scripture Hymn Title	UMH	MVPC	CLUW	TFWS	SOZ
We Sing to You, O God				2001	
Let All Things Now Living				2008	
Let Us with a Joyful Mind				2012	
Bless His Holy Name				2015	
We Bring the Sacrifice of Praise				2031	
Give Thanks				2036	
Nothing Can Trouble				2054	
Praise the Name of Jesus				2066	
All Who Hunger				2126	
You Who Are Thirsty				2132	
Why Stand So Far Away, My God?				2180	
How Long, O Lord				2209	
Lead On, O Cloud of Presence				2234	
Come to the Table				2264	

Colossians 3:1-11

Scripture Hymn Title	UMH	MVPC	CLUW	TFWS	SOZ
Holy God, We Praise Thy Name	79		80		
Now Thank We All Our God	102				
Christ the Lord Is Risen Today	302	152	193		
The Day of Resurrection	303		188		
Easter People, Raise Your Voices	304				6
O Jesus, I Have Promised	396	214			
Seek Ye First the Kingdom of God	405	201	136		
Close to Thee	407				7
Thou My Everlasting Portion	407				7
I Want a Principle Within	410				
In Christ there Is No East or West	548				65
Where Charity and Love Prevail	549				
Christ, From Whom All Blessings Flow	550		250		
The Church of Christ, in Every Age	589				
We Know that Christ Is Raised	610		231		
I Come with Joy to Meet My Lord	617				
One Bread, One Body	620	324	237		
Sing with All the Saints in Glory	702		382		
Let Us with a Joyful Mind				2012	
My Life Is in You, Lord				2032	
Woke Up This Morning				2082	
I Have Decided to Follow Jesus				2129	

Scripture Hymn Title	UMH	MVPC	CLUW	TFWS	SOZ
Change My Heart, O God				2152	
Jesus, Draw Me Close				2159	
To Know You More				2161	
Who Is My Mother, Who Is My Brother				2225	
Wonder of Wonders				2247	
Baptized in Water				2248	
Come, Share the Lord				2269	
Glory to God in the Highest				2276	

Luke 12:13-21

Scripture Hymn Title	UMH	MVPC	CLUW	TFWS	SOZ
There's a Spirit in the Air	192				
Nothing Between My Soul and My Savior	373				21
Take My Life, and Let It Be Consecrated	399		312		
Seek Ye First the Kingdom of God	405	201	136		
Close to Thee	407				7
Thou My Everlasting Portion	407				7
All Who Love and Serve Your City	433				
Cuando El Pobre Nada Tiene	434	301	138		
When the Poor Ones Who Have Nothing	434	301	138		
O God Who Shaped Creation	443				
If the World from You Withhold	522				23
Leave It There	522				23
Where Charity and Love Prevail	549				
Wake, Awake, for Night Is Flying	720				
Jesus, Draw Me Close				2159	

August 12, 2007 (Eleventh Sunday after Pentecost)

Scripture Hymn Title	UMH	MVPC	CLUW	TFWS	SOZ
Isaiah 1:1, 10-20					
Come Back Quickly to the Lord	343		272		
Just As I Am, Without One Plea	357				208
A Charge to Keep I Have	413				
The Voice of God Is Calling	436		139		
Let There Be Light	440				
What Does the Lord Require	441				
Creator of the Earth and Skies	450				
Jesus, Lover of My Soul	479				
The Church of Christ, in Every Age	589				
What Does the Lord Require of You				2174	
Wounded World that Cries for Healing				2177	
When God Restored Our Common Life				2182	
Song of Hope				2186	
Lord, Have Mercy				2277	
Psalm 50:1-8, 22-23					
Holy, Holy, Holy! Lord God Almighty	64	4	79		
Immortal, Invisible, God Only Wise	103		74		
Source and Sovereign, Rock and Cloud	113				
God of the Sparrow God of the Whale	122	37	59		
Seek the Lord Who Now Is Present	124				
O Morning Star, How Fair and Bright	247				
What Does the Lord Require	441				
Creator of the Earth and Skies	450				
From the Rising of the Sun				2024	
Praise to the Lord				2029	
We Bring the Sacrifice of Praise				2031	
Shine, Jesus, Shine				2173	

Scripture Hymn Title	UMH	MVPC	CLUW	TFWS	SOZ
Hebrews 11:1-3, 8-16					
Guide Me, O Thou Great Jehovah	127				
All My Hope Is Firmly Grounded	132				
Spirit of Faith, Come Down	332		219		
Let Us Plead for Faith Alone	385				
Through It All	507		279		
Faith, While Trees Are Still in Blossom	508		97		
Lift Every Voice and Sing	519				32
How Firm a Foundation	529	256			
Faith of Our Fathers	710	385			
I Know Not Why God's Wondrous Grace	714		290		
I Know Whom I Have Believed	714		290		
We Walk by Faith				2196	
Without Seeing You				2206	
Faith Is Patience in the Night				2211	
Deep in the Shadows of the Past				2246	
For All the Saints				2283	
Luke 12:32-40					
Give to the Winds Thy Fears	129		282		
Take Time to Be Holy	395				
Seek Ye First the Kingdom of God	405	201	136		
All Who Love and Serve Your City	433				
When the Poor Ones Who Have Nothing	434	301	138		
Cuando El Pobre Nada Tiene	434	301	138		
Move Me, Move Me	471		357		185
Lift Every Voice and Sing	519				32
How Firm a Foundation	529	256			
I Know Not Why God's Wondrous Grace	714		290		
I Know Whom I Have Believed	714		290		
My Lord, What a Morning	719		386		145
I Want to Be Ready	722				151
O Day of God, Draw Nigh	730				
All I Need Is You				2080	
Since Jesus Came Into My Heart				2140	
Jesus, Draw Me Close				2159	
You Are Mine				2218	

August 19, 2007 (Twelfth Sunday after Pentecost)

Scripture Hymn Title	UMH	MVPC	CLUW	TFWS	SOZ
Isaiah 5:1-7					
O God of Every Nation	435				
O God Who Shaped Creation	443				
Creator of the Earth and Skies	450				
Wellspring of Wisdom	506				
O Day of God, Draw Nigh	730				
Out of the Depths				2136	
God, How Can We Forgive				2169	
Wounded World that Cries for Healing				2177	
Unsettled World				2183	
Psalm 80:1-2, 8-19					
O God in Heaven, Grant to Thy Children	119		227		
Send Your Word	195		113		
O Come, O Come, Emmanuel	211	80			
O God of Every Nation	435				
O God Who Shaped Creation	443				
Creator of the Earth and Skies	450				
Wellspring of Wisdom	506				
God of Grace and God of Glory	577	287			
O Day of God, Draw Nigh	730				
Out of the Depths				2136	
Wounded World that Cries for Healing				2177	
Unsettled World				2183	
Hebrews 11:29–12:2					
Holy God, We Praise Thy Name	79		80		
O God in Heaven, Grant to Thy Children	119		227		
I Want to Walk As a Child of the Light	206		102		
Jesus, Keep Me Near the Cross	301				19

Scripture Hymn Title	UMH	MVPC	CLUW	TFWS	SOZ
Christ the Lord Is Risen Today	302	152	193		
Hail, Thou Once Despised Jesus	325				
The Head That Once Was Crowned with Thorns	326				
Let Us Plead for Faith Alone	385				
Am I a Soldier of the Cross	511				
By Gracious Powers So Wonderfully Sheltered	517				
How Firm a Foundation	529	256			
God of Grace and God of Glory	577	287			
Soon and Very Soon	706		385		198
Rejoice in God's Saints	708				
Faith of Our Fathers	710	385			
For All the Saints, Who from Their Labors Rest	711	384	388		
I Sing a Song of the Saints of God	712				
O What Their Joy and Their Glory Must Be	727				
He Who Began a Good Work in You				2163	
Guide My Feet				2208	
Faith Is Patience in the Night				2211	
In the Midst of New Dimensions				2238	
Deep in the Shadows of the Past				2246	
May You Run and Not Be Weary				2281	
For All the Saints				2283	

Luke 12:49-56

Scripture Hymn Title	UMH	MVPC	CLUW	TFWS	SOZ
If Thou But Suffer God to Guide Thee	142				
Am I a Soldier of the Cross	511				
By Gracious Powers So Wonderfully Sheltered	517				
How Firm a Foundation	529	256			
See How Great a Flame Aspires	541	248			
God of Love and God of Power	578				
Abide with Me; Fast Falls the Eventide	700				
O Day of God, Draw Nigh	730				
Swiftly Pass the Clouds of Glory				2102	
My Life Flows On				2212	

August 26, 2007 (Thirteenth Sunday after Pentecost)

Scripture Hymn Title	UMH	MVPC	CLUW	TFWS	SOZ
Jeremiah 1:4-10					
Morning Glory, Starlit Sky	194				
Of All the Spirit's Gifts to Me	336				
O Master, Let Me Walk with Thee	430		315		
Lord, Speak to Me, That I May Speak	463				
Send Me, Lord	497		331		
Whom Shall I Send?	582				
Here I Am, Lord	593	289	263		
I, the Lord of Sea and Sky	593	289	263		
How Shall They Hear the Word of God	649				
Womb of Life				2046	
Mothering God, You Gave Me Birth				2050	
I Was There to Hear Your Borning Cry				2051	
The Lone, Wild Bird				2052	
Spirit of God				2117	
Loving Spirit				2123	
Oh, I Know the Lord's Laid His Hands on Me				2139	
We Are Called				2172	
Psalm 71:1-6					
Now Thank We All Our God	102				
A Mighty Fortress Is Our God	110	25			
O God, Our Help in Ages Past	117				
All My Hope Is Firmly Grounded	132				
Leaning on the Everlasting Arms	133	244	291		53
What a Fellowship, What a Joy Divine	133	244	291		53
Praise to the Lord, the Almighty	139	29	68		
Rock of Ages, Cleft for Me	361	247			

Scripture Hymn Title	UMH	MVPC	CLUW	TFWS	SOZ
Saranam, Saranam	523		105		
Jesus, Savior, Lord, Lo, to Thee I Fly	523		105		
We Sing to You, O God				2001	
I Will Call Upon the Lord				2002	
Praise You				2003	
My Life Is in You, Lord				2032	
Mothering God, You Gave Me Birth				2050	
I Was There to Hear Your Borning Cry				2051	
Praise the Name of Jesus				2066	
Lord of All Hopefulness				2197	

Hebrews 12:18-29

Scripture Hymn Title	UMH	MVPC	CLUW	TFWS	SOZ
Immortal, Invisible, God Only Wise	103		74		
Steal Away to Jesus	704		378		134
O Holy City, Seen of John	726		390		
Glorious Things of Thee Are Spoken	731		256		
Come, We That Love the Lord (St. Thomas)	732				
Come, We That Love the Lord (Marching to Zion)	733				3
We're Marching to Zion	733				3
O God Beyond All Praising				2009	
We Sing of Your Glory				2011	
Holy, Holy				2039	
Awesome God				2040	

Luke 13:10-17

Scripture Hymn Title	UMH	MVPC	CLUW	TFWS	SOZ
I Danced in the Morning	261	128	170		
Lord of the Dance	261	128	170		
Heal Me, Hands of Jesus	262				
When Jesus the Healer Passed through Galilee	263		171		
Heal Us, Emmanuel, Hear Our Prayer	266		328		
Jesus' Hands Were Kind Hands	273		176		
O Master, Let Me Walk with Thee	430		315		
O Young and Fearless Prophet	444				
This Is the Day, This Is the Day (This Is the Day)	657				
This Is the Day the Lord Hath Made	658				

Scripture	Hymn Title	UMH	MVPC	CLUW	TFWS	SOZ
	Jesus, We Want to Meet	661				
	O Lord, You're Beautiful				2064	
	Oh, I Know the Lord's Laid His Hands on Me				2139	
	I'm So Glad Jesus Lifted Me				2151	
	Healer of Our Every Ill				2213	
	People Need the Lord				2244	

September 2, 2007 (Fourteenth Sunday after Pentecost)

Scripture Hymn Title	UMH	MVPC	CLUW	TFWS	SOZ
Jeremiah 2:4-13					
Seek the Lord Who Now Is Present	124				
Canticle of Covenant Faithfulness	125				
God Created Heaven and Earth	151				
We Utter Our Cry	439				
O God Who Shaped Creation	443				
Creator of the Earth and Skies	450				
How Shall They Hear the Word of God	649				
God Weeps				2048	
You Who Are Thirsty				2132	
We Are Called				2172	
Psalm 81:1, 10-16					
Praise the Lord Who Reigns Above	96		124		
O God Who Shaped Creation	443				
Creator of the Earth and Skies	450				
I, the Lord of Sea and Sky	593	289	263		
You Satisfy the Hungry Heart	629				
Lord God, Almighty				2006	
Nothing Can Trouble				2054	
Shout to the Lord				2074	
You Who Are Thirsty				2132	
Someone Asked the Question				2144	
We Are Called				2172	
The Trees of the Field				2279	
Hebrews 13:1-8, 15-16					
For the Beauty of the Earth	92	8			
A Mighty Fortress Is Our God	110	25			
All My Hope Is Firmly Grounded	132				

Scripture	Hymn Title	UMH	MVPC	CLUW	TFWS	SOZ
	If Thou But Suffer God to Guide Thee	142				
	There's a Spirit in the Air	192				
	Forgive Our Sins as We Forgive	390				
	O Jesus, I Have Promised	396	214			
	Jesu, Jesu, Fill Us with Your Love	432	288	179		
	Jesus, Savior, Lord, Lo, to Thee I Fly	523		105		
	Saranam, Saranam	523		105		
	How Firm a Foundation	529	256			
	Where Charity and Love Prevail	549				
	Blest Be the Tie that Binds	557	347			
	Jesus, United By Thy Grace	561				
	Lord God, Your Love Has Called Us Here	579				
	O Perfect Love, All Human Thought Transcending	645				
	O God Beyond All Praising				2009	
	We Bring the Sacrifice of Praise				2031	
	Carol of the Epiphany				2094	
	The Summons				2130	
	Together We Serve				2175	
	Make Me a Servant				2176	
	Here Am I				2178	
	Live in Charity				2179	
	We Need a Faith				2181	
	Now It Is Evening				2187	
	In Remembrance of Me				2254	
	As We Gather at Your Table				2268	
	Come, Share the Lord				2269	

Luke 14:1, 7-14

Scripture	Hymn Title	UMH	MVPC	CLUW	TFWS	SOZ
	All Praise to Thee, for Thou, O King Divine	166				
	Canticle of Christ's Obedience	167				
	Morning Glory, Starlit Sky	194				
	Come, Sinners, to the Gospel Feast (Invitation)	339		88		
	Come, Ye Sinners, Poor and Needy	340				
	Come, All of You	350				
	Jesu, Jesu, Fill Us with Your Love	432	288	179		

Scripture	Hymn Title	UMH	MVPC	CLUW	TFWS	SOZ
	Christ for the World We Sing	568		260		
	Lord God, Your Love Has Called Us Here	579				
	Lord, Whose Love Through Humble Service	581				
	Come, Sinners, to the Gospel Feast (Communion)	616				
	Humble Thyself in the Sight of the Lord				2131	
	Blest Are they				2155	
	Together We Serve				2175	
	Make Me a Servant				2176	
	Lord of All Hopefulness				2197	
	The Servant Song				2222	
	Gather Us In				2236	
	In Remembrance of Me				2254	
	Broken for Me				2263	
	Time Now to Gather				2265	
	As We Gather at Your Table				2268	

September 9, 2007 (Fifteenth Sunday after Pentecost)

Scripture Hymn Title	UMH	MVPC	CLUW	TFWS	SOZ
Jeremiah 18:1-11					
Have Thine Own Way, Lord	382	213	327		
Spirit of the Living God, Fall Afresh on Me	393	177	214		226
Take My Life, and Let It Be Consecrated	399		312		
My Lord, What a Morning	719		386		145
Praise You				2003	
God the Sculptor of the Mountains				2060	
Spirit of God				2117	
Change My Heart, O God				2152	
As a Fire Is Meant for Burning				2237	
Water, River, Spirit, Grace				2253	
Psalm 139:1-6, 13-18					
I'll Praise My Maker While I've Breath	60		123		
Now Thank We All Our God	102				
Immortal, Invisible, God Only Wise	103		74		
Creating God, Your Fingers Trace	109				
How Like a Gentle Spirit	115		216		
The Care the Eagle Gives Her Young	118		302		
Sing Praise to God Who Reigns Above	126		60		
Praise to the Lord, the Almighty	139	29	68		
Dear Lord, Lead Me Day by Day	411		100		
Thou Hidden Love of God	414				
Forth in Thy Name, O Lord, I Go	438				
Mothering God, You Gave Me Birth				2050	
I Was There to Hear Your Borning Cry				2051	
The Lone, Wild Bird				2052	
God the Sculptor of the Mountains				2060	
Loving Spirit				2123	
Guide My Feet				2208	

Scripture Hymn Title	UMH	MVPC	CLUW	TFWS	SOZ
Lead Me, Guide Me				2214	
You Are Mine				2218	

Philemon 1-21

Your Love, O God	120	26			
Go Down, Moses	448				112
In Christ there Is No East or West	548				65
Where Charity and Love Prevail	549				
Awake, O Sleeper, Rise from Death	551				
Help Us Accept Each Other	560		253		
Jesus, Lord, We Look to Thee	562				
Over My Head				2148	
Together We Serve				2175	
Live in Charity				2179	
Let Us Be Bread				2260	

Luke 14:25-33

Lift High the Cross	159	164	174		
Rejoice, Ye Pure in Heart (Marion)	160		130		
Rejoice, Ye Pure in Heart (Vineyard Haven)	161				
In the Cross of Christ I Glory	295				
I Can Hear My Savior Calling	338				42
Where He Leads Me	338				42
Take Up Thy Cross, the Savior Said	415		145		
Must Jesus Bear the Cross Alone	424				
Happy the Home When God Is there	445				
More Love to Thee, O Christ	453		318		
Am I a Soldier of the Cross	511				
Are Ye Able, Said the Master	530	300			
And Are We Yet Alive	553				
This Little Light of Mine	585		338		132
For the Bread Which You Have Broken (Beng-Li)	615				
O How He Loves You and Me				2108	
I Have Decided to Follow Jesus				2129	
Would I Have Answered When You Called				2137	
Cry of My Heart				2165	
You Are Mine				2218	
Let Us Be Bread				2260	

September 16, 2007 (Sixteenth Sunday after Pentecost)

Scripture Hymn Title	UMH	MVPC	CLUW	TFWS	SOZ
Jeremiah 4:11-12, 22-28					
La Palabra Del Señor Es Recta	107				
Righteous and Just Is the Word of Our Lord	107				
It's Me, It's Me, O Lord	352		326		110
Standing in the Need of Prayer	352		326		110
Creator of the Earth and Skies	450				
Steal Away to Jesus	704		378		134
My Lord, What a Morning	719		386		145
O Day of God, Draw Nigh	730				
Thou Art Worthy				2041	
God Weeps				2048	
Psalm 14					
We Believe in One True God	85				
La Palabra Del Señor Es Recta	107				
Righteous and Just Is the Word of Our Lord	107				
Seek the Lord Who Now Is Present	124				
Amazing Grace! How Sweet the Sound	378	203	94		211
Creator of the Earth and Skies	450				
Jesus, Savior, Lord, Lo, to Thee I Fly	523		105		
Saranam, Saranam	523		105		
Abide with Me; Fast Falls the Eventide	700				
Steal Away to Jesus	704		378		134
My Lord, What a Morning	719		386		145
O Day of God, Draw Nigh	730				
Bless the Lord				2013	
Honor and Praise				2018	

Scripture	Hymn Title	UMH	MVPC	CLUW	TFWS	SOZ
	God Weeps				2048	
	If It Had Not Been for the Lord				2053	
	Holy Spirit, Come to Us				2118	
	Humble Thyself in the Sight of the Lord				2131	
1 Timothy 1:12-17						
	Immortal, Invisible, God Only Wise	103		74		
	Hope of the World	178				
	Alas! and Did My Savior Bleed	294				8
	Depth of Mercy! Can There Be	355		273		
	Alas! and Did My Savior Bleed	359	202			8
	And Can It Be that I Should Gain	363	206	280		
	Grace Greater than Our Sin	365				
	Marvelous Grace of Our Loving Lord	365				
	My Hope Is Built on Nothing Less	368	261			
	I Stand Amazed in the Presence	371		93		
	Amazing Grace! How Sweet the Sound	378	203	94		211
	Something Beautiful, Something Good	394		303		
	Come, Thou Fount of Every Blessing	400	42	127		
	The First Song of Isaiah				2030	
	Glory to God				2033	
	If It Had Not Been for the Lord				2053	
	God Is So Good				2056	
	There Are Some Things I May Not Know				2147	
	Grace Alone				2162	
	Faith Is Patience in the Night				2211	
	Sing Alleluia to the Lord				2258	
Luke 15:1-10						
	Source and Sovereign, Rock and Cloud	113				
	How Like a Gentle Spirit	115		216		
	The King of Love My Shepherd Is	138				
	Rise, Shine, You People	187				
	Come, Sinners, to the Gospel Feast (Invitation)	339		88		
	I Sought the Lord, and Afterward I Knew	341				
	Softly and Tenderly Jesus Is Calling	348	193	284		
	Savior, Like a Shepherd Lead Us	381				

Scripture Hymn Title	UMH	MVPC	CLUW	TFWS	SOZ
Come, Thou Fount of Every Blessing	400	42	127		
The Voice of God Is Calling	436		139		
O God Who Shaped Creation	443				
Prayer Is the Soul's Sincere Desire	492				
Come, Sinners, to the Gospel Feast (Communion)	616				
Steal Away to Jesus	704		378		134
My Lord, What a Morning	719		386		145
Come, We That Love the Lord (St. Thomas)	732				
Come, We That Love the Lord (Marching to Zion)	733				3
We're Marching to Zion	733				3
The First Song of Isaiah				2030	
God Is So Good				2056	
I'm So Glad Jesus Lifted Me				2151	
Joy Comes with the Dawn				2210	

September 23, 2007 (Seventeenth Sunday after Pentecost)

Scripture Hymn Title	UMH	MVPC	CLUW	TFWS	SOZ
Jeremiah 8:18–9:1					
Dear Lord and Father of Mankind	358				
There Is a Balm in Gilead	375	262	98		123
I Want a Principle Within	410				
Behold a Broken World	426				
All Who Love and Serve Your City	433				
O God Who Shaped Creation	443				
There Is a Place of Quiet Rest	472		324		
Near to the Heart of God	472		324		
Jesus, Lover of My Soul	479				
O Love That Wilt Not Let Me Go	480	255	322		
O Thou, in Whose Presence My Soul Takes Delight	518				
What Does the Lord Require of You				2174	
Wounded World that Cries for Healing				2177	
Why Stand So Far Away, My God?				2180	
Lord of All Hopefulness				2197	
Psalm 79:1-9					
Dear Lord and Father of Mankind	358				
I Want a Principle Within	410				
Behold a Broken World	426				
All Who Love and Serve Your City	433				
O God of Every Nation	435				
Let There Be Light	440				
O Thou, in Whose Presence My Soul Takes Delight	518				
Wounded World that Cries for Healing				2177	
Why Stand So Far Away, My God?				2180	
How Long, O Lord				2209	

Scripture Hymn Title	UMH	MVPC	CLUW	TFWS	SOZ
1 Timothy 2:1-7					
We Believe in One True God	85				
God of Many Names	105				
Christ Is the World's Light	188				
Dona Nobis Pacem	376	360	142		
This Is My Song	437				
Let There Be Light	440				
Give Thanks				2036	
Jesus, Name Above All Names				2071	
Come and Find the Quiet Center				2128	
Make Me a Channel of Your Peace				2171	
Luke 16:1-13					
O Jesus, My King and My Sovereign	180	54			
Jesús Es Mi Rey Soberano	180	54			
I Surrender All	354	225			67
Nothing Between My Soul and My Savior	373				21
Jesus Calls Us o'er the Tumult	398		96		
Take My Life, and Let It Be Consecrated	399		312		
Seek Ye First the Kingdom of God	405	201	136		
All Who Love and Serve Your City	433				
Forth in Thy Name, O Lord, I Go	438				
What Does the Lord Require	441				
More Love to Thee, O Christ	453		318		
As the Deer				2025	
My Gratitude Now Accept, O Lord				2044	
More Precious than Silver				2065	
Jesus, Name Above All Names				2071	
Living for Jesus				2149	
We Are Called				2172	
What Does the Lord Require of You				2174	

September 30, 2007 (Eighteenth Sunday after Pentecost)

Scripture Hymn Title	UMH	MVPC	CLUW	TFWS	SOZ
Jeremiah 32:1-3a, 6-15					
O God, Our Help in Ages Past	117				
By Gracious Powers So Wonderfully Sheltered	517				
O Thou, in Whose Presence My Soul Takes Delight	518				
Be Still, My Soul	534		307		
Let All Things Now Living				2008	
If It Had Not Been for the Lord				2053	
Psalm 91:1-6, 14-16					
A Mighty Fortress Is Our God	110	25			
Be Not Dismayed Whate'er Betide	130	260			
God Will Take Care of You	130	260			
Children of the Heavenly Father	141		335		
On Eagle's Wings	143		83		
When Peace, Like a River, Attendeth My Way	377	250	304		20
It Is Well With My Soul	377	250	304		20
My Prayer Rises to Heaven	498				
Thy Holy Wings, O Savior	502				
By Gracious Powers So Wonderfully Sheltered	517				
O Thou, in Whose Presence My Soul Takes Delight	518				
Saranam, Saranam	523	105			
Jesus, Savior, Lord, Lo, to Thee I Fly	523	105			
We Sing to You, O God				2001	
I Will Call Upon the Lord				2002	
Sing a New Song to the Lord				2045	

Scripture Hymn Title	UMH	MVPC	CLUW	TFWS	SOZ
If It Had Not Been for the Lord				2053	
Nothing Can Trouble				2054	
You Are My Hiding Place				2055	
Praise the Name of Jesus				2066	
Shout to the Lord				2074	
Holy Spirit, Come to Us				2118	
O Holy Spirit, Root of Life				2121	
Blessed Quietness				2142	

1 Timothy 6:6-19

Scripture Hymn Title	UMH	MVPC	CLUW	TFWS	SOZ
Come, Thou Almighty King	61	11			
Immortal, Invisible, God Only Wise	103		74		
All My Hope Is Firmly Grounded	132				
Pues Si Vivimos	356	337	310		
Take Time to Be Holy	395				
Take My Life, and Let It Be Consecrated	399		312		
Dear Lord, Lead Me Day by Day	411		100		
A Charge to Keep I Have	413				
When Our Confidence Is Shaken	505				
Stand Up, Stand Up for Jesus	514				
Are Ye Able, Said the Master	530	300			
Faith of Our Fathers	710	385			
I Sing a Song of the Saints of God	712				
Nothing Can Trouble				2054	
All Hail King Jesus				2069	
King of Kings				2075	
We Will Glorify the King of Kings				2087	
Christ the Lord Has Risen				2116	
The Summons				2130	
He Who Began a Good Work in You				2163	
More Like You				2167	
Faith Is Patience in the Night				2211	

Luke 16:19-31

Scripture Hymn Title	UMH	MVPC	CLUW	TFWS	SOZ
Cuando El Pobre Nada Tiene	434	301	138		
When the Poor Ones Who Have Nothing	434	301	138		
The Voice of God Is Calling	436		139		
We Utter Our Cry	439				

Scripture	Hymn Title	UMH	MVPC	CLUW	TFWS	SOZ
	What Does the Lord Require	441				
	Go Down, Moses	448				112
	Are Ye Able, Said the Master	530	300			
	When the Church of Jesus Shuts Its Outer Door	592				
	Blessed Jesus, at Thy Word	596		108		
	Fix Me, Jesus	655				122
	I Sing a Song of the Saints of God	712				
	Give Thanks				2036	
	My Gratitude Now Accept, O Lord				2044	
	We Are Called				2172	
	What Does the Lord Require of You				2174	
	Here Am I				2178	

October 7, 2007 (Ninettenth Sunday after Pentecost)

Scripture Hymn Title	UMH	MVPC	CLUW	TFWS	SOZ
Lamentations 1:1-6					
It's Me, It's Me, O Lord	352		326		110
Standing in the Need of Prayer	352		326		110
Dear Lord,for All in Pain	458				
My Prayer Rises to Heaven	498				
O Thou, in Whose Presence My Soul Takes Delight	518				
Saranam, Saranam	523		105		
Jesus, Savior, Lord, Lo, to Thee I Fly	523		105		
Psalm 137					
My Prayer Rises to Heaven	498				
Come, Ye Disconsolate, Where'er Ye Languish	510				
I Love Thy Kingdom, Lord	540				
Someone Asked the Question				2144	
Come and Fill Our Hearts				2157	
When We Are Called to Sing Your Praise				2216	
By the Babylonian Rivers				2217	
2 Timothy 1:1-14					
Christ Jesus Lay in Death's Strong Bands	319				
Standing on the Promises of Christ My King	374	252			
My Faith Looks Up to Thee	452				215
Holy Spirit, Truth Divine	465				
O Thou Who Camest From Above	501		269		
When Our Confidence Is Shaken	505				

Scripture Hymn Title	UMH	MVPC	CLUW	TFWS	SOZ
Am I a Soldier of the Cross	511				
Stand Up, Stand Up for Jesus	514				
By Gracious Powers So Wonderfully Sheltered	517				
Jesus, Priceless Treasure	532				
Forward Through the Ages	555				
Draw Us in the Spirit's Tether	632				
I Know Not Why God's Wondrous Grace	714		290		
I Know Whom I Have Believed	714		290		
He (God) Who Began a Good Work in You				2163	
Cry of My Heart				2165	
Faith Is Patience in the Night				2211	
In the Singing				2255	
Here Is Bread, Here Is Wine				2266	

Luke 17:5-10

Scripture Hymn Title	UMH	MVPC	CLUW	TFWS	SOZ
Let Us Plead for Faith Alone	385				
Close to Thee	407				7
Thou My Everlasting Portion	407				7
Forth in Thy Name, O Lord, I Go	438				
My Faith Looks Up to Thee	452				215
My God, I Love Thee	470				
When Our Confidence Is Shaken	505				
Faith, While Trees Are Still in Blossom	508	97			
By Gracious Powers So Wonderfully Sheltered	517				
God of Love and God of Power	578				
Give Me the Faith Which Can Remove	650				
We Need a Faith				2181	
Faith Is Patience in the Night				2211	

October 8, 2007 (Thanksgiving Day, Canada)

Scripture Hymn Title	UMH	MVPC	CLUW	TFWS	SOZ
Deuteronomy 26:1-11					
Praise, My Soul, the King of Heaven	66				
What Gift Can We Bring	87				
For the Fruits of This Creation	97				
God, Whose Love Is Reigning o'er Us	100		73		
The God of Abraham Praise	116	28			
Praise to the Lord, the Almighty	139	29	68		
Come, Ye Thankful People, Come	694		241		
God of the Ages	698	377			
O God Beyond All Praising				2009	
How Majestic Is Your Name				2023	
We Bring the Sacrifice of Praise				2031	
Lead On, O Cloud of Presence				2234	
In the Midst of New Dimensions				2238	
Psalm 100					
I'll Praise My Maker While I've Breath	60		123		
Blessed Be the Name	63				
Canticle of Thanksgiving	74				
All People That on Earth Do Dwell	75		118		
Praise God, from Whom All Blessings Flow (Lasst)	94	167	352		
Praise God, from Whom All Blessings Flow (Old)	95	21			
God, Whose Love Is Reigning o'er Us	100		73		
Now Thank We All Our God	102				
Sing Praise to God Who Reigns Above	126		60		
I Sing the Almighty Power of God	152		65		
Savior, Like a Shepherd Lead Us	381				

Scripture	Hymn Title	UMH	MVPC	CLUW	TFWS	SOZ
	For the Healing of the Nations	428				
	Come, Ye Thankful People, Come	694		241		
	Let All Things Now Living				2008	
	Come, Rejoice in God				2017	
	Halle, Halle, Halleluja				2026	
	Give Thanks				2036	
	Father, I Adore You				2038	
	He Is Exalted				2070	
	Shout to the Lord				2074	
	In the Lord I'll Be Ever Thankful				2195	
	He Has Made Me Glad				2270	
	Come, All You People				2274	

Philippians 4:4-9

Scripture	Hymn Title	UMH	MVPC	CLUW	TFWS	SOZ
	Thank You, Lord	84				228
	God of the Sparrow God of the Whale	122	37	59		
	Sing Praise to God Who Reigns Above	126		60		
	Rejoice, Ye Pure in Heart (Marion)	160		130		
	Rejoice, Ye Pure in Heart (Vineyard Haven)	161				
	Tell Out, My Soul, the Greatness of the Lord!	200				
	Good Christian Friends, Rejoice	224		155		
	Sweet Hour of Prayer	496	248	330		
	O Thou, in Whose Presence My Soul Takes Delight	518				
	What a Friend We Have in Jesus	526	257	333		
	Where Charity and Love Prevail	549				
	Jesus, United By Thy Grace	561				
	Jesus, Lord, We Look to Thee	562				
	Savior, Again to Thy Dear Name	663	349			
	Go Now in Peace	665		363		
	Rejoice, the Lord Is King (Darwall's 148th)	715				
	Rejoice, the Lord Is King (Gopsal)	716				
	Come, Rejoice in God				2017	
	Give Thanks				2036	
	I've Got Peace Like a River				2145	
	Give Peace				2156	
	Come and Fill Our Hearts				2157	
	Sanctuary				2164	

Scripture Hymn Title	UMH	MVPC	CLUW	TFWS	SOZ
Make Me a Channel of Your Peace				2171	
Lord of All Hopefulness				2197	
Cares Chorus				2215	
In the Singing				2255	
Let Us Offer to the Father				2262	

John 6:25-35

Scripture Hymn Title	UMH	MVPC	CLUW	TFWS	SOZ
Guide Me, O Thou Great Jehovah	127				
Come, Sinners, to the Gospel Feast (Invitation)	339		88		
Cuando El Pobre Nada Tiene	434	301	138		
When the Poor Ones Who Have Nothing	434	301	138		
Forth in Thy Name, O Lord, I Go	438				
Blessed Jesus, at Thy Word	596		108		
Break Thou the Bread of Life	599				
Deck Thyself, My Soul, with Gladness	612				
Come, Sinners, to the Gospel Feast (Communion)	616				
Let Us Break Bread Together	618	316	236		88
Here, O My Lord, I See Thee	623				
Bread of the World in Mercy Broken	624		240		
Come, Let Us Eat	625				
Eat This Bread, Drink This Cup	628				
You Satisfy the Hungry Heart	629				
Become to Us the Living Bread	630				
O Food to Pilgrims Given	631				
Fill My Cup, Lord	641				
Jesus, Joy of Our Desiring	644		344		
Mothering God, You Gave Me Birth				2050	
God the Sculptor of the Mountains				2060	
The Lily of the Valley				2062	
Jesus, Name Above All Names				2071	
Light of the World				2204	
Gather Us In				2236	
Let Us Be Bread				2260	
Life-giving Bread				2261	
As We Gather at Your Table				2268	

October 14, 2007 (Twentieth Sunday after Pentecost)

Scripture Hymn Title	UMH	MVPC	CLUW	TFWS	SOZ
Jeremiah 29:1, 4-7					
All Who Love and Serve Your City	433				
Not So in Haste, My Heart	455				
O Thou, in Whose Presence My Soul Takes Delight	518				
Lift Every Voice and Sing	519				32
We Need a Faith				2181	
When God Restored Our Common Life				2182	
Unsettled World				2183	
Song of Hope				2186	
When We Are Called to Sing Your Praise				2216	
Psalm 66:1-12					
O for a Thousand Tongues to Sing	57	1	226		
Blessed Be the Name	63				
Praise, My Soul, the King of Heaven	66				
We, Thy People, Praise Thee	67		72		
¡Canta, Débora, Canta!	81				
¡Canta, Débora, Canta!	81				
Joyful, Joyful, We Adore Thee	89	5	75		
Let All the World in Every Corner Sing	93				
To God Be the Glory, Great Things He Hath Done!	98	169	78		
From All That Dwell Below the Skies	101		126		
O Thou, in Whose Presence My Soul Takes Delight	518				
Lift Every Voice and Sing	519				32
How Firm a Foundation	529	256			
We Sing to You, O God				2001	
Lord God, Almighty				2006	

Scripture Hymn Title	UMH	MVPC	CLUW	TFWS	SOZ
We Sing of Your Glory				2011	
Awesome God				2040	
Shout to the Lord				2074	
Come and See				2127	
Someone Asked the Question				2144	

2 Timothy 2:8-15

Lift High the Cross	159	164	174		
In the Cross of Christ I Glory	295				
Easter People, Raise Your Voices	304				6
The Head That Once Was Crowned with Thorns	326				
Must Jesus Bear the Cross Alone	424				
Lord, Speak to Me, That I May Speak	463				
Am I a Soldier of the Cross	511				
Stand Up, Stand Up for Jesus	514				
Are Ye Able, Said the Master	530	300			
Jesus, Priceless Treasure	532				
Be Still, My Soul	534		307		
God of Grace and God of Glory	577	287			
All Hail King Jesus				2069	
Lord, I Lift Your Name on High				2088	

Luke 17:11-19

I'll Praise My Maker While I've Breath	60		123		
Praise, My Soul, the King of Heaven	66				
We, Thy People, Praise Thee	67		72		
We Would See Jesus	256		168		
Heal Me, Hands of Jesus	262				
When Jesus the Healer Passed Through Galilee	263		171		
O Christ, the Healer, We Have Come	265				
Jesus' Hands Were Kind Hands	273		176		
How Can We Sinners Know	372		288		
There Is a Balm in Gilead	375	262	98		123
Something Beautiful, Something Good	394		303		
Dear Lord, for All in Pain	458				
Awake, O Sleeper, Rise from Death	551				
Give Thanks				2036	

Scripture	Hymn Title	UMH	MVPC	CLUW	TFWS	SOZ
	Thank You, Jesus				2081	
	An Outcast Among Outcasts				2104	
	In the Lord I'll Be Ever Thankful				2195	
	Healer of Our Every Ill				2213	

October 21, 2007 (Twenty-first Sunday after Pentecost)

Scripture Hymn Title	UMH	MVPC	CLUW	TFWS	SOZ
Jeremiah 31:27-34					
Great Is Thy Faithfulness	140	30	81		
If Thou But Suffer God to Guide Thee	142				
All Earth Is Waiting to See the Promised One	210	78			
Toda la Tierra Espera al Salvador	210	78			
This Is a Day of New Beginnings	383	208	311		
I Want a Principle Within	410				
Breathe on Me, Breath of God	420				
O Love That Wilt Not Let Me Go	480	255	322		
Sois la Semilla	583	291			
You Are the Seed	583	291			
Here I Am, Lord	593	289	263		
I, the Lord of Sea and Sky	593	289	263		
Come, Let Us Use the Grace Divine	606				
God Is So Good				2056	
God the Sculptor of the Mountains				2060	
Give Me a Clean Heart				2133	
Change My Heart, O God				2152	
Please Enter My Heart, Hosanna				2154	
Come and Fill Our Hearts				2157	
Wonder of Wonders				2247	
Life-giving Bread				2261	
Psalm 119:97-104					
O Master, Let Me Walk with Thee	430		315		
O Word of God Incarnate	598				
Wonderful Words of Life	600	313			
Sing Them over Again to Me	600	313			

Scripture Hymn Title	UMH	MVPC	CLUW	TFWS	SOZ
Thy Word Is a Lamp unto My Feet	601		109		
O Lord, May Church and Home Combine	695				
As the Deer				2025	
More Precious than Silver				2065	
Cry of My Heart				2165	

2 Timothy 3:14–4:5

	UMH	MVPC	CLUW	TFWS	SOZ
Holy God, We Praise Thy Name	79		80		
O Master, Let Me Walk with Thee	430		315		
Lord, Speak to Me, That I May Speak	463				
Through It All	507		279		
Lord, You Give the Great Commission	584				
O Word of God Incarnate	598				
Thy Word Is a Lamp unto My Feet	601		109		
Come, Holy Ghost, Our Hearts Inspire	603		218		
Faith of Our Fathers	710	385			
I Know Not Why God's Wondrous Grace	714		290		
I Know Whom I Have Believed	714		290		
Praise the Source of Faith and Learning				2004	
Deep in the Shadows of the Past				2246	

Luke 18:1-8

	UMH	MVPC	CLUW	TFWS	SOZ
It's Me, It's Me, O Lord	352		326		110
Standing in the Need of Prayer	352		326		110
Be Thou My Vision	451	240			
Not So in Haste, My Heart	455				
I Will Trust in the Lord	464		292		14
Remember Me, Remember Me	491		234		235
Prayer Is the Soul's Sincere Desire	492				
Kum Ba Yah, My Lord	494		332		139
Sweet Hour of Prayer	496	248	330		
Leave It There	522				23
If the World from You Withhold	522				23
What a Friend We Have in Jesus	526	257	333		
Do, Lord, Remember Me	527				119
Lord, Listen to Your Children Praying				2193	
Lord, Listen to Your Children				2207	

October 28, 2007 (Twenty-second Sunday after Pentecost)

Scripture Hymn Title	UMH	MVPC	CLUW	TFWS	SOZ
Joel 2:23-32					
We, Thy People, Praise Thee	67		72		
Depth of Mercy! Can there Be	355		273		
Spirit of the Living God, Fall Afresh on Me	393	177	214		226
Spirit of God, Descend Upon My Heart	500				
Wind Who Makes All Winds that Blow	538				
See How Great a Flame Aspires	541		248		
You Satisfy the Hungry Heart	629				
Come, Holy Ghost, Our Souls Inspire	651				
O Day of Peace that Dimly Shines	729				
Now Praise the Hidden Love of God				2027	
Spirit, Spirit of Gentleness				2120	
Come, O Holy Spirit, Come				2124	
Healer of Our Every Ill				2213	
Lead On, O Cloud of Presence				2234	
Deep in the Shadows of the Past				2246	
Psalm 65					
All Creatures of Our God and King	62	22			
Mountains Are All Aglow	86				
For the Beauty of the Earth	92	8			
For the Fruits of This Creation	97				
Sing Praise to God Who Reigns Above	126		60		
We Gather Together to Ask the Lord's Blessing	131	361			
All My Hope Is Firmly Grounded	132				
Praise to the Lord, the Almighty	139	29	68		
I Sing the Almighty Power of God	152		65		
Come, Christians, Join to Sing	158				

Scripture	Hymn Title	UMH	MVPC	CLUW	TFWS	SOZ
	Una Espiga	637	319			
	Lord, Dismiss Us with Thy Blessing	671				
	Rise to Greet the Sun	678		371		
	America the Beautiful	696				
	O Beautiful for Spacious Skies	696				
	Awesome God				2040	
	Thou Art Worthy				2041	
	Sing a New Song to the Lord				2045	
	Praise Our God Above				2061	
	The Trees of the Field				2279	

2 Timothy 4:6-8, 16-18

Scripture	Hymn Title	UMH	MVPC	CLUW	TFWS	SOZ
	And Can It Be that I Should Gain	363	206	280		
	O Love That Wilt Not Let Me Go	480	255	322		
	When Our Confidence Is Shaken	505				
	Through It All	507		279		
	Stand by Me	512				41
	When the Storms of Life Are Raging	512				41
	Stand Up, Stand Up for Jesus	514				
	What a Friend We Have in Jesus	526	257	333		
	How Firm a Foundation	529	256			
	And Are We Yet Alive	553				
	Lead On, O King Eternal	580	174			
	Abide With Me; Fast Falls the Eventide	700				
	Come, Let Us Join Our Friends Above	709		387		
	Faith of Our Fathers	710	385			
	For All the Saints, Who from Their Labors Rest	711	384	388		
	Humble Thyself in the Sight of the Lord				2131	
	He Who Began a Good Work in You				2163	
	Guide My Feet				2208	
	Faith Is Patience in the Night				2211	

Luke 18:9-14

Scripture	Hymn Title	UMH	MVPC	CLUW	TFWS	SOZ
	Pass Me Not, O Gentle Savior	351		271		
	It's Me, It's Me, O Lord	352		326		110
	Standing in the Need of Prayer	352		326		110
	Depth of Mercy! Can there Be	355		273		

Scripture	Hymn Title	UMH	MVPC	CLUW	TFWS	SOZ
	Just As I Am, Without One Plea	357				208
	Rock of Ages, Cleft for Me	361	247			
	I Stand Amazed in the Presence	371		93		
	I Am Thine, O Lord	419	218			
	The Lily of the Valley				2062	
	Humble Thyself in the Sight of the Lord				2131	
	Forgive Us, Lord				2134	

November 1, 2007 (All Saints)

May also be used Sunday, November 4, 2007

Scripture Hymn Title	UMH	MVPC	CLUW	TFWS	SOZ
Daniel 7:1-3, 15-18					
Come, Thou Almighty King	61	11			
Beams of Heaven As I Go	524				10, 207
We Are Tossed and Driven on the Restless Sea of Time	525	317			
We'll Understand It Better By and By	525	317			55
Come, Let Us Join Our Friends Above	709		387		
For All the Saints, Who from Their Labors Rest	711	384	388		
In His Time				2203	
Psalm 149					
All Creatures of Our God and King	62	22			
How Great Thou Art	77	2	61		
Canticle of the Holy Trinity, Response	80				
Ye Watchers and Ye Holy Ones	90				
Praise the Lord Who Reigns Above	96		124		
Praise to the Lord, the Almighty	139	29	68		
Cantemos Al Señor	149	49	67		
Let's Sing unto the Lord	149	49	67		
Rejoice, the Lord Is King (Darwall's 148th)	715				
Let All Things Now Living				2008	
Come, Rejoice in God				2017	
Clap Your Hands				2028	
We Bring the Sacrifice of Praise				2031	
Give Thanks				2036	
Sing a New Song to the Lord				2045	

Scripture	Hymn Title	UMH	MVPC	CLUW	TFWS	SOZ
	I Love You, Lord				2068	
	Shout to the Lord				2074	
	Humble Thyself in the Sight of the Lord				2131	
	He Who Began a Good Work in You				2163	
	He Has Made Me Glad				2270	

Ephesians 1:11-23

Scripture	Hymn Title	UMH	MVPC	CLUW	TFWS	SOZ
	When in Our Music God Is Glorified	68		129		
	If Thou But Suffer God to Guide Thee	142				
	All Hail the Power of Jesus' Name (Coronation)	154	60			
	All Hail the Power of Jesus' Name (Diadem)	155				
	Jesus Shall Reign Where'er the Sun	157				
	His Name Is Wonderful	174	172	203		
	Hope of the World	178				
	Hail, Thou Once Despised Jesus	325				
	The Head That Once Was Crowned with Thorns	326				
	Crown Him With Many Crowns	327	157			
	My Hope Is Built on Nothing Less	368	261			
	Come, Thou Fount of Every Blessing	400	42	127		
	Lift Every Voice and Sing	519				32
	Come, Let Us Join Our Friends Above	709		387		
	Faith of Our Fathers	710	385			
	For All the Saints, Who from Their Labors Rest	711	384	388		
	You Are Worthy				2063	
	Open Our Eyes				2086	
	Loving Spirit				2123	
	There Are Some Things I May Not Know				2147	
	I'm Gonna Live So God Can Use Me				2153	
	He Who Began a Good Work in You				2163	
	The Fragrance of Christ				2205	
	We Are God's People				2220	
	In Unity We Lift Our Song				2221	
	Baptized in Water				2248	
	Life-giving Bread				2261	

Scripture	Hymn Title	UMH	MVPC	CLUW	TFWS	SOZ
	Come, Share the Lord				2269	
	Glory to God in the Highest				2276	
	The Trees of the Field				2279	

Luke 6:20-31

Scripture	Hymn Title	UMH	MVPC	CLUW	TFWS	SOZ
	If Thou But Suffer God to Guide Thee	142				
	Lift Every Voice and Sing	519				32
	Nobody Knows the Trouble I See	520				170
	How Firm a Foundation	529	256			
	Hymn of Promise	707	338	392		
	In the Bulb There Is a Flower	707	338	392		
	Faith of Our Fathers	710	385			
	Come Sunday	728				
	Holy				2019	
	Give Thanks				2036	
	Blest Are they				2155	
	For All the Saints				2283	

November 4, 2007 (Twenty-third Sunday after Pentecost)

May also use readings and hymns for November 1, 2007, All Saints Day

Scripture Hymn Title	UMH	MVPC	CLUW	TFWS	SOZ
Habakkuk 1:1-4; 2:1-4					
Creator of the Earth and Skies	450				
Be Thou My Vision	451	240			
Not So in Haste, My Heart	455				
When Our Confidence Is Shaken	505				
We Are Tossed and Driven on the Restless Sea of Time	525	317			55
We'll Understand It Better By and By	525	317			55
Be Still, My Soul	534		307		
O Holy City, Seen of John	726		390		
O What their Joy and their Glory Must Be	727				
O Day of God, Draw Nigh	730				
The Lily of the Valley				2062	
Psalm 119:137-144					
Righteous and Just Is the Word of Our Lord	107				
La Palabra Del Señor Es Recta	107				
Break Thou the Bread of Life	599				
Thy Word Is a Lamp unto My Feet	601		109		
O Lord, May Church and Home Combine	695				
To Know You More				2161	
Cry of My Heart				2165	
2 Thessalonians 1:1-4, 11-12					
A Charge to Keep I Have	413				
Be Still, My Soul	534		307		
Where Charity and Love Prevail	549				

Scripture Hymn Title	UMH	MVPC	CLUW	TFWS	SOZ
Jesus, Lord, We Look to Thee	562				
How Blest Are They Who Trust in Christ	654				
Stand Up and Bless the Lord	662		128		
Give Thanks				2036	
Lord, Be Glorified				2150	
He Who Began a Good Work in You				2163	
One God and Father of Us All				2240	

Luke 19:1-10

	UMH	MVPC	CLUW	TFWS	SOZ
Jesus, the Very Thought of Thee	175				
Jesús Es Mi Rey Soberano	180	54			
O Jesus, My King and My Sovereign	180	54			
Heal Me, Hands of Jesus	262				
Jesus' Hands Were Kind Hands	273		176		
Come, Sinners, to the Gospel Feast (Invitation)	339		88		
Come, Ye Sinners, Poor and Needy	340				
I Sought the Lord, and Afterward I Knew	341				
O Let the Son of God Enfold You	347	190	91		
Spirit Song	347	190	91		
Amazing Grace! How Sweet the Sound	378	203	94		211
I Am Thine, O Lord	419	218			
Cuando El Pobre Nada Tiene	434	301	138		
When the Poor Ones Who Have Nothing	434	301	138		
Our Parent, by Whose Name	447				
Rescue the Perishing	591				
Come, Sinners, to the Gospel Feast (Communion)	616				
I Come with Joy to Meet My Lord	617				
Living for Jesus				2149	
Cry of My Heart				2165	
When God Restored Our Common Life				2182	

November 11, 2007 (Twenty-fourth Sunday after Pentecost)

Scripture Hymn Title	UMH	MVPC	CLUW	TFWS	SOZ
Haggai 1:15b–2:9					
Come, Thou Long-Expected Jesus	196	82			
O Come, O Come, Emmanuel	211	80			
Take My Life, and Let It Be Consecrated	399		312		
Saranam, Saranam	523		105		
Jesus, Savior, Lord, Lo, to Thee I Fly	523		105		
Rise Up, O Men of God	576				
God of Love and God of Power	578				
Jesus, Joy of Our Desiring	644		344		
Glorious Things of Thee Are Spoken	731		256		
Lord, Listen to Your Children Praying				2193	
Psalm 145:1-5, 17-21					
O for a Thousand Tongues to Sing	57	1	226		
Mil Voces Para Celebrar	59				
All Creatures of Our God and King	62	22			
Blessed Be the Name	63				
Praise, My Soul, the King of Heaven	66				
How Great Thou Art	77	2	61		
O Lord My God! When I in Awesome Wonder	77	2	61		
Canticle of the Holy Trinity, Response	80				
Joyful, Joyful, We Adore Thee	89	5	75		
Let All the World in Every Corner Sing	93				
Praise to the Lord, the Almighty	139	29	68		
Children of the Heavenly Father	141		335		
Ye Servants of God, Your Master Proclaim	181				
Let All Things Now Living				2008	

Scripture Hymn Title	UMH	MVPC	CLUW	TFWS	SOZ
O God Beyond All Praising				2009	
Great Is the Lord				2022	
I Sing Praises to Your Name				2037	
Awesome God				2040	
He Is Exalted				2070	
Lord, I Lift Your Name on High				2088	

2 Thessalonians 2:1-5, 13-17

For the Fruits of This Creation	97				
All Who Love and Serve Your City	433				
Forth in Thy Name, O Lord, I Go	438				
Christ, From Whom All Blessings Flow	550		250		
Soon and Very Soon	706		385		198
Blessed Quietness				2142	

Luke 20:27-38

I'll Praise My Maker While I've Breath	60		123		
Immortal, Invisible, God Only Wise	103		74		
The God of Abraham Praise	116	28			
Children of the Heavenly Father	141		335		
Christ Is Risen! Shout Hosanna	307				
Standing on the Promises of Christ My King	374	252			
Spirit of the Living God, Fall Afresh on Me	393	177	214		226
And Are We Yet Alive	553				
Christ the Victorious, Give to Your Servants	653		380		
God Is Here	660				
Sent Forth By God's Blessing	664		366		
When We All Get to Heaven	701	383	381		15
Sing the Wondrous Love of Jesus	701	383	381		15
Sing with All the Saints in Glory	702		382		
Come, Let Us Join Our Friends Above	709		387		
Let All Things Now Living				2008	
Lord, I Lift Your Name on High				2088	
Living for Jesus				2149	
We Are God's People				2220	

November 18, 2007 (Twenty-fifth Sunday after Pentecost)

Scripture Hymn Title	UMH	MVPC	CLUW	TFWS	SOZ
Isaiah 65:17-25					
Camina, Pueblo De Dios	305	151			
Walk On, O People of God	305	151			
Come, Ye Faithful, Raise the Strain	315				
This Is a Day of New Beginnings	383	208	311		
Behold a Broken World	426				
We Know That Christ Is Raised	610		231		
O Day of Peace that Dimly Shines	729				
Come, We That Love the Lord (Marching to Zion)	733				3
We're Marching to Zion	733				3
Canticle of Hope, Response	734				
I'll Fly Away				2282	
Joy in the Morning				2284	
Isaiah 12					
O for a Thousand Tongues to Sing	57	1	226		
Mil Voces Para Celebrar	59				
Let All the World in Every Corner Sing	93				
From All That Dwell Below the Skies	101		126		
Cantemos al Señor	149	49	67		
Let's Sing unto the Lord	149	49	67		
Rejoice, Ye Pure in Heart (Marion)	160		130		
Alleluia	186		355		
Tell Out, My Soul, the Greatness of the Lord!	200				
I Will Trust in the Lord	464		292		14
Stand Up and Bless the Lord	662		128		
O Day of God, Draw Nigh	730				
Praise to the Lord				2029	

Scripture	Hymn Title	UMH	MVPC	CLUW	TFWS	SOZ
	The First Song of Isaiah				2030	
	My Life Is in You, Lord				2032	
	Give Thanks				2036	
	He Is Exalted				2070	
	Shout to the Lord				2074	
	Someone Asked the Question				2144	
	In the Lord I'll Be Ever Thankful				2195	
	Cares Chorus				2215	
	The Trees of the Field				2279	

Psalm 118

Scripture	Hymn Title	UMH	MVPC	CLUW	TFWS	SOZ
	Heleluyan, Heleluyan	78	39	354		
	My Tribute	99				
	Praise to the Lord, the Almighty	139	29	68		
	In Thee Is Gladness	169				
	Alleluia	186		355		
	Good Christian Friends, Rejoice	224		155		
	Filled with Excitement, All the Happy Throng	279	136	178		
	All Glory, Laud, and Honor	280				
	The Day of Resurrection	303		188		
	Hail Thee, Festival Day	324				
	Christ Is Made the Sure Foundation	559				
	This Is the Day, This Is the Day	657				
	This Is the Day the Lord Hath Made	658				
	Stand Up and Bless the Lord	662		128		
	Let Us with a Joyful Mind				2012	
	Blessed Be the Name of the Lord				2034	
	Alleluia (Celtic)				2043	
	You Alone Are Holy				2077	
	Alleluia (Honduras)				2078	
	Thank You, Jesus				2081	
	Come, Let Us With Our Lord Arise				2084	
	The King of Glory Comes				2091	
	Hosanna! Hosanna!				2109	
	We Sang Our Glad Hosannas				2111	
	Holy, Holy, Holy Lord				2256	
	He Has Made Me Glad				2270	

Scripture Hymn Title	UMH	MVPC	CLUW	TFWS	SOZ

2 Thessalonians 3:6-13

Scripture Hymn Title	UMH	MVPC	CLUW	TFWS	SOZ
For the Fruits of This Creation	97				
All Who Love and Serve Your City	433				
Forth in Thy Name, O Lord, I Go	438				
Christ, from Whom All Blessings Flow	550		250		
Soon and Very Soon	706		385		198
Blessed Quietness				2142	

Luke 21:5-19

Scripture Hymn Title	UMH	MVPC	CLUW	TFWS	SOZ
When Peace, Like a River, Attendeth My Way	377	250	304		20
It Is Well With My Soul	377	250	304		20
O Crucified Redeemer	425				
Behold a Broken World	426				
Where Cross the Crowded Ways of Life	427	296			
All Who Love and Serve Your City	433				
We Utter Our Cry	439				
Creator of the Earth and Skies	450				
Lord, Speak to Me, That I May Speak	463				
Stand by Me	512				41
When the Storms of Life Are Raging	512				41
By Gracious Powers So Wonderfully Sheltered	517				
Lift Every Voice and Sing	519				32
How Firm a Foundation	529	256			
Praise and Thanksgiving Be to God	604		230		
Soon and Very Soon	706		385		198
O Day of Peace That Dimly Shines	729				
O Day of God, Draw Nigh	730				
Come, We That Love the Lord (Marching to Zion)	733				3
We're Marching to Zion	733				3
Blessed Quietness				2142	
Freedom Is Coming				2192	
O Freedom				2194	

November 22, 2007 (Thanksgiving Day, U.S.A.)

Scripture Hymn Title	UMH	MVPC	CLUW	TFWS	SOZ
Deuteronomy 26:1-11					
Praise, My Soul, the King of Heaven	66				
What Gift Can We Bring	87				
For the Fruits of This Creation	97				
God, Whose Love Is Reigning o'er Us	100		73		
The God of Abraham Praise	116	28			
Praise to the Lord, the Almighty	139	29	68		
Come, Ye Thankful People, Come	694		241		
God of the Ages	698	377			
O God Beyond All Praising				2009	
How Majestic Is Your Name				2023	
We Bring the Sacrifice of Praise				2031	
Lead On, O Cloud of Presence				2234	
In the Midst of New Dimensions				2238	
Psalm 100					
I'll Praise My Maker While I've Breath	60		123		
Blessed Be the Name	63				
Canticle of Thanksgiving	74				
All People That on Earth Do Dwell	75		118		
Praise God, from Whom All Blessings Flow (Lasst	94	167	352		
Praise God, from Whom All Blessings Flow (Old	95	21			
God, Whose Love Is Reigning o'er Us	100		73		
Now Thank We All Our God	102				
Sing Praise to God Who Reigns Above	126		60		
I Sing the Almighty Power of God	152		65		
Savior, Like a Shepherd Lead Us	381				
For the Healing of the Nations	428				

Scripture Hymn Title	UMH	MVPC	CLUW	TFWS	SOZ
Come, Ye Thankful People, Come	694		241		
Let All Things Now Living				2008	
Come, Rejoice in God				2017	
Halle, Halle, Halleluja				2026	
Give Thanks				2036	
Father, I Adore You				2038	
He Is Exalted				2070	
Shout to the Lord				2074	
In the Lord I'll Be Ever Thankful				2195	
He Has Made Me Glad				2270	
Come, All You People				2274	

Philippians 4:4-9

Scripture Hymn Title	UMH	MVPC	CLUW	TFWS	SOZ
Thank You, Lord	84				228
God of the Sparrow God of the Whale	122	37	59		
Sing Praise to God Who Reigns Above	126		60		
Rejoice, Ye Pure in Heart (Marion)	160		130		
Rejoice, Ye Pure in Heart (Vineyard Haven)	161				
Tell Out, My Soul, the Greatness of the Lord!	200				
Good Christian Friends, Rejoice	224		155		
Sweet Hour of Prayer	496	248	330		
O Thou, in Whose Presence My Soul Takes Delight	518				
What a Friend We Have in Jesus	526	257	333		
Where Charity and Love Prevail	549				
Jesus, United By Thy Grace	561				
Jesus, Lord, We Look to Thee	562				
Savior, Again to Thy Dear Name	663	349			
Go Now in Peace	665		363		
Rejoice, the Lord Is King (Darwall's 148th)	715				
Rejoice, the Lord Is King (Gopsal)	716				
Come, Rejoice in God				2017	
Give Thanks				2036	
I've Got Peace Like a River				2145	
Give Peace				2156	

Scripture Hymn Title	UMH	MVPC	CLUW	TFWS	SOZ
Come and Fill Our Hearts				2157	
Sanctuary				2164	
Make Me a Channel of Your Peace				2171	
Lord of All Hopefulness				2197	
Cares Chorus				2215	
In the Singing				2255	
Let Us Offer to the Father				2262	

John 6:25-35

Scripture Hymn Title	UMH	MVPC	CLUW	TFWS	SOZ
Guide Me, O Thou Great Jehovah	127				
Come, Sinners, to the Gospel Feast (Invitation)	339		88		
Cuando El Pobre Nada Tiene	434	301	138		
When the Poor Ones Who Have Nothing	434	301	138		
Forth in Thy Name, O Lord, I Go	438				
Blessed Jesus, at Thy Word	596		108		
Break Thou the Bread of Life	599				
Deck Thyself, My Soul, with Gladness	612				
Come, Sinners, to the Gospel Feast (Communion)	616				
Let Us Break Bread Together	618	316	236		88
Here, O My Lord, I See Thee	623				
Bread of the World in Mercy Broken	624		240		
Come, Let Us Eat	625				
Eat This Bread, Drink This Cup	628				
You Satisfy the Hungry Heart	629				
Become to Us the Living Bread	630				
O Food to Pilgrims Given	631				
Fill My Cup, Lord	641				
Jesus, Joy of Our Desiring	644		344		
Mothering God, You Gave Me Birth				2050	
God the Sculptor of the Mountains				2060	
The Lily of the Valley				2062	
Jesus, Name Above All Names				2071	
Light of the World				2204	
Gather Us In				2236	
Let Us Be Bread				2260	
Life-giving Bread				2261	
As We Gather at Your Table				2268	

November 25, 2007 (Christ the King/Reign of Christ)

Scripture Hymn Title	UMH	MVPC	CLUW	TFWS	SOZ
Jeremiah 23:1-6					
Jesus Shall Reign Where'er the Sun	157				
Savior, Like a Shepherd Lead Us	381				
God the Spirit, Guide and Guardian	648				
Give Me the Faith Which Can Remove	650				
Sing a New Song to the Lord				2045	
We Will Glorify the King of Kings				2087	
Wounded World that Cries for Healing				2177	
Unsettled World				2183	
Sent Out in Jesus' Name				2184	
Luke 1:68-79					
Christ, Whose Glory, Fills the Skies	173		281		
Christ Is the World's Light	188				
People, Look East	202				
I Want to Walk as a Child of the Light	206		102		
Canticle of Zechariah, Response	208				
Blessed Be the God of Israel	209				
O Come, O Come, Emmanuel	211	80			
Lo, How a Rose E'er Blooming	216				
Break Forth, O Beauteous Heavenly Light	223				
Sing of Mary, Pure and Lowly	272				
Heralds of Christ, Who Bear the King's Commands	567				
Come, Let Us Eat	625				
Come, and Let Us Sweetly Join	699				
Awesome God				2040	
He Came Down				2085	
She Comes Sailing on the Wind				2122	
Blessed Quietness				2142	

Scripture Hymn Title	UMH	MVPC	CLUW	TFWS	SOZ
We Are Called				2172	
Shine, Jesus, Shine				2173	
Now It Is Evening				2187	
Light of the World				2204	
Guide My Feet				2208	
Lead Me, Guide Me				2214	
We Are Singing/We Are Marching				2235	
Gather Us In				2236	
In the Singing				2255	
Here Is Bread, Here Is Wine				2266	
As We Gather at Your Table				2268	

Colossians 1:11-20

Scripture Hymn Title	UMH	MVPC	CLUW	TFWS	SOZ
Immortal, Invisible, God Only Wise	103		74		
Alleluia, Alleluia! Give Thanks to the Risen Lord	162				
At the Name of Jesus Every Knee Shall Bow	168				
His Name Is Wonderful	174	172	203		
Of the Father's Love Begotten	184	52	66		
Rise, Shine, You People	187				
Sing, My Tongue, the Glorious Battle	296				
Beneath the Cross of Jesus	297				
Jesus, Keep Me Near the Cross	301				19
The Strife Is O'er, the Battle Done	306				
Christ Is Made the Sure Foundation	559				
O Splendor of God's Glory Bright	679				
Give Thanks				2036	
Thou Art Worthy				2041	
Jesus, Name Above All Names				2071	
I've Got Peace Like a River				2145	
Shine, Jesus, Shine				2173	
We Need a Faith				2181	
In the Lord I'll Be Ever Thankful				2195	
We Are God's People				2220	
Life-giving Bread				2261	
Come, Share the Lord				2269	
May You Run and Not Be Weary				2281	

Scripture Hymn Title	UMH	MVPC	CLUW	TFWS	SOZ
Luke 23:33-43					
I Danced in the Morning	261	128	170		
Lord of the Dance	261	128	170		
Sing, My Tongue, the Glorious Battle	296				
Beneath the Cross of Jesus	297				
Hail, Thou Once Despised Jesus	325				
Crown Him With Many Crowns	327	157			
Victory in Jesus	370		92		
I Heard an Old, Old Story	370		92		
Forgive Our Sins as We Forgive	390				
Jesus, Remember Me	488	249	364		
Remember Me, Remember Me	491		234		235
Do, Lord, Remember Me	527				119
Lord, You Give the Great Commission	584				
When Jesus Wept				2106	
Lamb of God				2113	

December 2, 2007 (First Sunday of Advent)

Scripture Hymn Title	UMH	MVPC	CLUW	TFWS	SOZ
Isaiah 2:1-5					
The God of Abraham Praise	116	28			
God of the Sparrow God of the Whale	122	37	59		
There's Something About That Name	171	74			
I Want to Walk as a Child of the Light	206		102		
Dona Nobis Pacem	376	360	142		
Behold a Broken World	426				
For the Healing of the Nations	428				
O God of Every Nation	435				
This Is My Song	437				
Let There Be Light	440				
We've a Story to Tell to the Nations	569				
God Be with You till We Meet Again (God Be With You)	672		347		37
God Be With You Till We Meet Again (Randolph)	673				
Soon and Very Soon	706		385		198
O Day of Peace that Dimly Shines	729				
O Day of God, Draw Nigh	730				
Someone Asked the Question				2144	
We Are Called				2172	
Freedom Is Coming				2192	
In the Lord I'll Be Ever Thankful				2195	
Light of the World				2204	
Lead Me, Guide Me				2214	
Come Now, O Prince of Peace				2232	
We Are Singing/We Are Marching				2235	
He Has Made Me Glad				2270	

Scripture Hymn Title	UMH	MVPC	CLUW	TFWS	SOZ
Psalm 122					
O Come, O Come, Emmanuel	211	80			
All Who Love and Serve Your City	433				
Shalom Chaverim	667	351	362		
Arise, Shine Out, Your Light Has Come	725				
O Day of God, Draw Nigh	730				
Glorious Things of Thee Are Spoken	731		256		
Give Peace				2156	
In the Lord I'll Be Ever Thankful				2195	
He Has Made Me Glad				2270	
Romans 13:11-14					
Come, Thou Long-Expected Jesus	196	82			
People, Look East	202				
I Want to Walk as a Child of the Light	206		102		
Awake, O Sleeper, Rise From Death	551				
Now Let Us from This Table Rise	634				
Father, We Praise Thee, Now the Night Is Over	680				
My Lord, What a Morning	719		386		145
Wake, Awake, for Night Is Flying	720				
Arise, Shine				2005	
Like a Child				2092	
Light of the World				2204	
Lead Me, Guide Me				2214	
Gather Us In				2236	
Matthew 24:36-44					
There's Something About that Name	171	74			
Send Your Word	195		113		
Come, Thou Long-Expected Jesus	196	82			
People, Look East	202				
Soon and Very Soon	706		385		198
I Know Not Why God's Wondrous Grace	714		290		
I Know Whom I Have Believed	714		290		
Rejoice, the Lord Is King (Gopsal)	716				
My Lord, What a Morning	719		386		145
Wake, Awake, for Night Is Flying	720				

Scripture Hymn Title	UMH	MVPC	CLUW	TFWS	SOZ
I Want to Be Ready	722				151
The King of Glory Comes				2091	
Freedom Is Coming				2192	
We Are Singing/We Are Marching				2235	

December 9, 2007 (Second Sunday of Advent)

Scripture Hymn Title	UMH	MVPC	CLUW	TFWS	SOZ
Isaiah 11:1-10					
Come, Thou Long-Expected Jesus	196	82			
Hail to the Lord's Anointed	203	81			
Blessed Be the God of Israel	209				
Toda La Tierra Espera Al Salvador	210	78			
All Earth Is Waiting to See the Promised One	210	78			
O Come, O Come, Emmanuel	211	80			
Savior of the Nations, Come	214				
Lo, How a Rose E'er Blooming	216				
O Morning Star, How Fair and Bright	247				
Spirit of God, Descend Upon My Heart	500				
I Come With Joy to Meet My Lord	617				
Come, Holy Ghost, Our Souls Inspire	651				
O Day of Peace That Dimly Shines	729				
O Day of God, Draw Nigh	730				
He Came Down				2085	
The King of Glory Comes				2091	
Like a Child				2092	
Star-Child				2095	
He Who Began a Good Work in You				2163	
Psalm 72:1-7, 18-19					
Blessed Be the Name	63				
Seek the Lord Who Now Is Present	124				
Jesus Shall Reign Where'Er the Sun	157				
Send Your Word	195		113		
Hail to the Lord's Anointed	203	81			

Scripture	Hymn Title	UMH	MVPC	CLUW	TFWS	SOZ
	Lift Up Your Heads, Ye Mighty Gates	213				
	Blessed Be the Name of the Lord				2034	
	He Came Down				2085	
	Holy Spirit, Come to Us				2118	
	Wounded World that Cries for Healing				2177	
	Here Am I				2178	
	When God Restored Our Common Life				2182	
	Song of Hope				2186	
Romans 15:4-13						
	Hope of the World	178				
	Come, Thou Long-Expected Jesus	196	82			
	Hail to the Lord's Anointed	203	81			
	O Morning Star, How Fair and Bright	247				
	O Let the Son of God Enfold You	347	190	91		
	Spirit Song	347	190	91		
	O Church of God, United	547		249		
	Help Us Accept Each Other	560		253		
	Jesus, United By Thy Grace	561				
	Blest Be the Dear Uniting Love	566		254		
	Go Now in Peace	665		363		
	Lord, Dismiss Us with Thy Blessing	671				
	Glorify Thy Name				2016	
	He Came Down				2085	
	Blessed Quietness				2142	
	Together We Serve				2175	
	Song of Hope				2186	
	Lord of All Hopefulness				2197	
	You Are Mine				2218	
	Come Now, O Prince of Peace				2232	
Matthew 3:1-12						
	Alleluia	186		355		
	Prepare the Way of the Lord	207		141		
	Blessed Be the God of Israel	209				
	Toda La Tierra Espera Al Salvador	210	78			
	All Earth Is Waiting to See the Promised One	210	78			
	'Tis the Old Ship of Zion	345				131

Scripture	Hymn Title	UMH	MVPC	CLUW	TFWS	SOZ
	O Let the Son of God Enfold You	347	190	91		
	Spirit Song	347	190	91		
	It's Me, It's Me, O Lord	352		326		110
	Standing in the Need of Prayer	352		326		110
	Take My Life, and Let It Be Consecrated	399		312		
	A Charge to Keep I Have	413				
	Open My Eyes, that I May See	454	184			
	O Thou Who Camest from Above	501		269		
	Like the Murmur of the Dove's Song	544				
	Heralds of Christ, Who Bear the King's Commands	567				
	Come, Holy Ghost, Our Souls Inspire	651				
	God the Sculptor of the Mountains				2060	
	Jesus, Name Above All Names				2071	
	He Came Down				2085	
	Wild and Lone the Prophet's Voice				2089	
	Holy Spirit, Come to Us				2118	
	Song of Hope				2186	
	Come Now, O Prince of Peace				2232	

December 16, 2007 (Third Sunday of Advent)

Scripture Hymn Title	UMH	MVPC	CLUW	TFWS	SOZ
Isaiah 35:1-10					
O for a Thousand Tongues to Sing	57	1	226		
Mil Voces Para Celebrar	59				
I Want to Walk as a Child of the Light	206		102		
Blessed Be the God of Israel	209				
Lift Up Your Heads, Ye Mighty Gates	213				
Lo, How a Rose E'er Blooming	216				
It Came upon the Midnight Clear	218	90			
Good Christian Friends, Rejoice	224		155		
En El Frío Invernal	233				
Cold December Flies Away	233				
That Boy-Child of Mary	241				
O Master, Let Me Walk with Thee	430		315		
Heralds of Christ, Who Bear the King's Commands	567				
Come, We That Love the Lord (St. Thomas)	732				
Come, We That Love the Lord (Marching to Zion)	733				3
We're Marching to Zion	733				3
Arise, Shine				2005	
The First Song of Isaiah				2030	
Give Thanks				2036	
The King of Glory Comes				2091	
She Comes Sailing on the Wind				2122	
Joy Comes with the Dawn				2210	
In Unity We Lift Our Song				2221	
Joy in the Morning				2284	

Scripture Hymn Title	UMH	MVPC	CLUW	TFWS	SOZ
Psalm 146:5-10					
O for a Thousand Tongues to Sing	57	1	226		
Mil Voces Para Celebrar	59				
Hope of the World	178				
Tell Out, My Soul, the Greatness of the Lord	200				
Luke 1:47-55					
Ye Who Claim the Faith of Jesus	197				
My Soul Gives Glory to My God	198				
Canticle of Mary; Response	199				
Tell Out, My Soul, the Greatness of the Lord!	200				
People, Look East	202				
Hail to the Lord's Anointed	203	81			
Blessed Be the God of Israel	209				
O Come, O Come, Emmanuel	211	80			
Savior of the Nations, Come	214				
To a Maid Engaged to Joseph	215		151		
Lo, How a Rose E'er Blooming	216				
It Came upon the Midnight Clear	218	90			
In the Bleak Midwinter	221				
He Is Born, the Holy Child	228	117	156		
O Come, All Ye Faithful	234	106			
That Boy-Child of Mary	241				
Joy to the World, the Lord Is Come!	246	100	161		
Once in Royal David's City	250		159		
Sing of Mary, Pure and Lowly	272				
The First One Ever, Oh, Ever to Know	276				
When the Poor Ones Who Have Nothing	434	301	138		
Cuando El Pobre Nada Tiene	434	301	138		
What Does the Lord Require	441				
Arise, Shine				2005	
Bless His Holy Name				2015	
Praise to the Lord				2029	
The First Song of Isaiah				2030	
Glory to God				2033	

Scripture Hymn Title	UMH	MVPC	CLUW	TFWS	SOZ
Give Thanks				2036	
God Is So Good				2056	
The Snow Lay on the Ground				2093	
The Virgin Mary Had a Baby Boy				2098	
Joseph Dearest, Joseph Mine				2099	
She Comes Sailing on the Wind				2122	
I'm So Glad Jesus Lifted Me				2151	
Blest Are they				2155	
Freedom Is Coming				2192	
Holy Ground				2272	

James 5:7-10

	UMH	MVPC	CLUW	TFWS	SOZ
If Thou But Suffer God to Guide Thee	142				
Come, Thou Long-Expected Jesus	196	82			
I Want to Walk as a Child of the Light	206		102		
It Came upon the Midnight Clear	218	90			
Not So in Haste, My Heart	455				
Faith, While Trees Are Still in Blossom	508		97		
Be Still, My Soul	534		307		
Rejoice, the Lord Is King (Darwall's 148th)	715				
Rejoice, the Lord Is King (Gopsal)	716				
Freedom Is Coming				2192	
Faith Is Patience in the Night				2211	
In Unity We Lift Our Song				2221	

Matthew 11:2-11

	UMH	MVPC	CLUW	TFWS	SOZ
O For a Thousand Tongues to Sing	57	1	226		
Mil Voces Para Celebrar	59				
Word of God, Come Down on Earth	182				
Ye Who Claim the Faith of Jesus	197				
My Soul Gives Glory to My God	198				
Tell Out, My Soul, the Greatness of the Lord	200				
Hail to the Lord's Anointed	203	81			
Prepare the Way of the Lord	207		141		
Blessed Be the God of Israel	209				
It Came upon the Midnight Clear	218	90			
Good Christian Friends, Rejoice	224		155		
That Boy-Child of Mary	241				

Scripture	Hymn Title	UMH	MVPC	CLUW	TFWS	SOZ
	When Jesus the Healer Passed Through Galilee	263		171		
	When Our Confidence Is Shaken	505				
	Break Thou the Bread of Life	599				
	Praise to the Lord				2029	
	My Song Is Love Unknown				2083	
	He Came Down				2085	
	The Snow Lay on the Ground				2093	
	The Virgin Mary Had a Baby Boy				2098	
	She Comes Sailing on the Wind				2122	
	The Summons				2130	
	I'm So Glad Jesus Lifted Me				2151	
	Blest Are they				2155	
	Now It Is Evening				2187	
	Freedom Is Coming				2192	

December 23, 2007 (Fourth Sunday of Advent)

Scripture Hymn Title	UMH	MVPC	CLUW	TFWS	SOZ
Isaiah 7:10-16					
Emmanuel, Emmanuel, His Name Is Called	204	76	211		
I Want to Walk as a Child of the Light	206		102		
All Earth Is Waiting to See the Promised One	210	78			
Toda la Tierra Espera al Salvador	210	78			
O Come, O Come, Emmanuel	211	80			
Savior of the Nations, Come	214				
Hark! the Herald Angels Sing	240	101			
All Hail King Jesus				2069	
Jesus, Name above All Names				2071	
Like a Child				2092	
We Are Called				2172	
Psalm 80:1-7, 17-19					
O God in Heaven, Grant to Thy Children	119		227		
Great Is Thy Faithfulness	140	30	81		
Send Your Word	195		113		
Come, Thou Long-Expected Jesus	196	82			
People, Look East	202				
I Want to Walk as a Child of the Light	206		102		
O Come, O Come, Emmanuel	211	80			
Lift Up Your Heads, Ye Mighty Gates	213				
Nothing between My Soul and My Savior	373				21
O God of Every Nation	435				
O God Who Shaped Creation	443				
Creator of the Earth and Skies	450				
Wellspring of Wisdom	506				

Scripture Hymn Title	UMH	MVPC	CLUW	TFWS	SOZ
God of Grace and God of Glory	577	287			
Wake, Awake, for Night Is Flying	720				
O Day of God, Draw Nigh	730				
The First Song of Isaiah				2030	
Shepherd Me, O God				2058	
Out of the Depths				2136	
We Are Called				2172	
Shine, Jesus, Shine				2173	
Wounded World that Cries for Healing				2177	
Unsettled World				2183	
Lord, Listen to Your Children				2207	
Lead Me, Guide Me				2214	

Romans 1:1-7

Scripture Hymn Title	UMH	MVPC	CLUW	TFWS	SOZ
Alleluia, Alleluia! Give Thanks to the Risen Lord	162				
Rise, Shine, You People	187				
Jesus! the Name High over All	193		199		
Send Your Word	195		113		
Hail to the Lord's Anointed	203	81			
Blessed Be the God of Israel	209				
O Come, All Ye Faithful	234	106			
Thou Didst Leave Thy Throne				2100	
Make Me a Servant				2176	

Matthew 1:18-25

Scripture Hymn Title	UMH	MVPC	CLUW	TFWS	SOZ
At the Name of Jesus Every Knee Shall Bow	168				
There's Something About that Name	171	74			
Come, Thou Long-Expected Jesus	196	82			
Ye Who Claim the Faith of Jesus	197				
Emmanuel, Emmanuel, His Name Is Called	204	76	211		
All Earth Is Waiting to See the Promised One	210	78			
Toda la Tierra Espera al Salvador	210	78			
O Come, O Come, Emmanuel	211	80			
Savior of the Nations, Come	214				
To a Maid Engaged to Joseph	215		151		

Scripture Hymn Title	UMH	MVPC	CLUW	TFWS	SOZ
Lo, How a Rose E'er Blooming	216				
Angels from the Realms of Glory	220				
He Is Born, the Holy Child	228	117	156		
O Little Town of Bethlehem	230	94			
O Come, All Ye Faithful	234	106			
Rock-a-Bye, My Dear Little Boy	235				
Hark! the Herald Angels Sing	240	101			
That Boy-Child of Mary	241				
All Hail King Jesus				2069	
Jesus, Name Above All Names				2071	
The King of Glory Comes				2091	
Rise Up, Shepherd, and Follow				2096	
Joseph Dearest, Joseph Mine				2099	
Thou Didst Leave Thy Throne				2100	
O Holy Spirit, Root of Life				2121	
Gather Us In				2236	

December 24, 2007 (Christmas Eve)

Scripture Hymn Title	UMH	MVPC	CLUW	TFWS	SOZ
Isaiah 9:2-7					
The God of Abraham Praise	116	28			
Christ, Whose Glory Fills the Skies	173		281		
His Name Is Wonderful	174	172	203		
Come, Thou Long-Expected Jesus	196	82			
Canticle of Light and Darkness, Response 2	205				
I Want to Walk as a Child of the Light	206		102		
All Earth Is Waiting to See the Promised One	210	78			
Toda La Tierra Espera Al Salvador	210	78			
It Came Upon the Midnight Clear	218	90			
Break Forth, O Beauteous Heavenly Light	223				
O Come, All Ye Faithful	234	106			
Hark! the Herald Angels Sing	240	101			
O Morning Star, How Fair and Bright	247				
We've a Story to Tell to the Nations	569				
O Splendor of God's Glory Bright	679				
Arise, Shine Out, Your Light Has Come	725				
O Day of Peace That Dimly Shines	729				
What a Mighty God We Serve				2021	
How Majestic Is Your Name				2023	
Jesus, Name Above All Names				2071	
King of Kings				2075	
We Are Called				2172	
Shine, Jesus, Shine				2173	
Light of the World				2204	
Goodness Is Stronger than Evil				2219	

Scripture Hymn Title	UMH	MVPC	CLUW	TFWS	SOZ
Come Now, O Prince of Peace				2232	
Gather Us In				2236	

Psalm 96

Scripture Hymn Title	UMH	MVPC	CLUW	TFWS	SOZ
O for a Thousand Tongues to Sing	57	1	226		
Praise, My Soul, the King of Heaven	66				
How Great Thou Art	77	2	61		
O Lord My God! When I in Awesome Wonder	77	2	61		
Holy God, We Praise Thy Name	79		80		
Canticle of Praise to God	91				
Praise the Lord Who Reigns Above	96		124		
Majesty, Worship His Majesty	176	171	204		
Of the Father's Love Begotten	184	52	66		
In the Bleak Midwinter	221				
Sing We Now of Christmas	237		166		
Hark! the Herald Angels Sing	240	101			
On This Day Earth Shall Ring	248				
We Sing to You, O God				2001	
We Sing of Your Glory				2011	
Honor and Praise				2018	
Great Is the Lord				2022	
Praise, Praise, Praise the Lord				2035	
I Sing Praises to Your Name				2037	
Sing a New Song to the Lord				2045	
Amen, We Praise Your Name, O God				2067	
Shout to the Lord				2074	
King of Kings				2075	
Someone Asked the Question				2144	

Titus 2:11-14

Scripture Hymn Title	UMH	MVPC	CLUW	TFWS	SOZ
Come, Thou Long-Expected Jesus	196	82			
Break Forth, O Beauteous Heavenly Light	223				
Good Christian Friends, Rejoice	224		155		
Joy to the World, the Lord Is Come!	246	100	161		
On This Day Earth Shall Ring	248				
My Hope Is Built on Nothing Less	368	261			
Blessed Assurance, Jesus Is Mine!	369	65	287		

Scripture	Hymn Title	UMH	MVPC	CLUW	TFWS	SOZ
	I Need Thee Every Hour	397				
	I Want a Principle Within	410				
	A Charge to Keep I Have	413				
	O Master, Let Me Walk with Thee	430		315		
	I Love You, Lord				2068	
	Lord, I Lift Your Name on High				2088	
	Rise Up, Shepherd, and Follow				2096	
	Sing Alleluia to the Lord				2258	
	Here Is Bread, Here Is Wine				2266	

Luke 2:1-20

Scripture	Hymn Title	UMH	MVPC	CLUW	TFWS	SOZ
	Glory Be to the Father (Greatorex)	71				
	Gloria, Gloria in Excelsis Deo!	72		353		
	Holy God, We Praise Thy Name	79		80		
	Canticle of God's Glory; Response	83				
	Maker, in Whom We Live	88				
	Lift High the Cross	159	164	174		
	At the Name of Jesus Every Knee Shall Bow	168				
	O Sing a Song of Bethlehem	179				
	Of the Father's Love Begotten	184	52	66		
	Savior of the Nations, Come	214				
	Lo, How a Rose E'er Blooming	216				
	Away in a Manger	217	93	157		
	It Came upon the Midnight Clear	218	90			
	What Child Is This	219	112	154		
	Angels from the Realms of Glory	220				
	In the Bleak Midwinter	221				
	Child So Lovely, Here I Kneel Before You	222	114			
	Niño Lindo, Ante Ti Me Rindo	222	114			
	Break Forth, O Beauteous Heavenly Light	223				
	Good Christian Friends, Rejoice	224		155		
	The Friendly Beasts	227				
	Jesus, Our Brother, Strong and Good	227				
	Infant Holy, Infant Lowly	229	116	152		
	When Christmas Morn Is Dawning	232				

Scripture Hymn Title	UMH	MVPC	CLUW	TFWS	SOZ
While Shepherds Watched Their Flocks by Night	236				
Sing We Now of Christmas	237		166		
Angels We Have Heard on High	238	98			
Silent Night, Holy Night	239	103	160		
Hark! the Herald Angels Sing	240	101			
That Boy-Child of Mary	241				
The First Noel the Angel Did Say	245	89			
Joy to the World, the Lord Is Come!	246	100	161		
On This Day Earth Shall Ring	248				
Once in Royal David's City	250		159		
Go, Tell It on the Mountain	251	97			75
Woman in the Night	274				
Dona Nobis Pacem	376	360	142		
O Day of Peace That Dimly Shines	729				
We Sing of Your Glory				2011	
Come, Rejoice in God				2017	
Glory to God				2033	
I Sing Praises to Your Name				2037	
Amen, Amen				2072	
He Came Down				2085	
Lord, I Lift Your Name on High				2088	
Like a Child				2092	
The Snow Lay on the Ground				2093	
Star-Child				2095	
Rise Up, Shepherd, and Follow				2096	
One Holy Night in Bethlehem				2097	
The Virgin Mary Had a Baby Boy				2098	
Joseph Dearest, Joseph Mine				2099	
Thou Didst Leave Thy Throne				2100	
Spirit, Spirit of Gentleness				2120	
Come and See				2127	
Glory to God in the Highest				2276	

December 25, 2007 (Christmas Day)

Scripture Hymn Title	UMH	MVPC	CLUW	TFWS	SOZ
Isaiah 52:7-10					
Come, Thou Long-Expected Jesus	196	82			
Prepare the Way of the Lord	207		141		
Good Christian Friends, Rejoice	224		155		
Joy to the World, the Lord Is Come!	246	100	161		
Wake, Awake, for Night Is Flying	720				
Let Us with a Joyful Mind				2012	
Someone Asked the Question				2144	
Psalm 98					
All Creatures of Our God and King	62	22			
When in Our Music God Is Glorified	68		129		
Let All the World in Every Corner Sing	93				
Praise the Lord Who Reigns Above	96		124		
Children of the Heavenly Father	141		335		
Cantemos al Señor	149	49	67		
Let's Sing unto the Lord	149	49	67		
Joy to the World, the Lord Is Come	246	100	161		
Camina, Pueblo De Dios	305	151			
Walk On, O People of God	305	151			
The Strife Is O'er, the Battle Done	306				
The Head That Once Was Crowned With Thorns	326				
Praise the Lord with the Sound of Trumpet				2020	
Clap Your Hands				2028	
Sing a New Song to the Lord				2045	
Shout to the Lord				2074	
The Trees of the Field				2279	

181

Scripture Hymn Title	UMH	MVPC	CLUW	TFWS	SOZ
Hebrews 1:1-12					
Of the Father's Love Begotten	184	52	66		
He Is Born, the Holy Child	228	117	156		
O Come, All Ye Faithful	234	106			
Rock-a-Bye, My Dear Little Boy	235				
John 1:1-14					
Come, Thou Almighty King	61	11			
Morning Has Broken	145	354	370		
At the Name of Jesus Every Knee Shall Bow	168				
Christ, Whose Glory Fills the Skies	173		281		
Word of God, Come Down on Earth	182				
Of the Father's Love Begotten	184	52	66		
Christ Is the World's Light	188				
Send Your Word	195		113		
I Want to Walk as a Child of the Light	206		102		
Break Forth, O Beauteous Heavenly Light	223				
Good Christian Friends, Rejoice	224		155		
When Christmas Morn Is Dawning	232				
Cold December Flies Away	233				
En el Frío Invernal	233				
O Come, All Ye Faithful	234	106			
Hark! the Herald Angels Sing	240	101			
Love Came Down at Christmas	242				
Joy to the World, the Lord Is Come!	246	100	161		
O Morning Star, How Fair and Bright	247				
On This Day Earth Shall Ring	248				
Go, Tell It on the Mountain	251	97			75
Sing of Mary, Pure and Lowly	272				
Hail, Thou Once Despised Jesus	325				
O Love That Wilt Not Let Me Go	480	255	322		
O Word of God Incarnate	598				
Jesus, Joy of Our Desiring	644		344		
Now, on Land and Sea Descending	685		372		
Thou Art Worthy				2041	
Womb of Life				2046	

Scripture Hymn Title	UMH	MVPC	CLUW	TFWS	SOZ
Mothering God, You Gave Me Birth				2050	
I Was There to Hear Your Borning Cry				2051	
Jesus, Name Above All Names				2071	
Lord, I Lift Your Name on High				2088	
Thou Didst Leave Thy Throne				2100	
Christ the Lord Has Risen				2116	
O Holy Spirit, Root of Life				2121	
Shine, Jesus, Shine				2173	
Now It Is Evening				2187	
Light of the World				2204	
We Are Singing/We Are Marching				2235a-b	

December 30, 2007 (First Sunday after Christmas Day)

Scripture Hymn Title	UMH	MVPC	CLUW	TFWS	SOZ
Isaiah 63:7-9					
Sing Praise to God Who Reigns Above	126		60		
Praise to the Lord, the Almighty	139	29	68		
Great Is Thy Faithfulness	140	30	81		
Children of the Heavenly Father	141		335		
In Thee Is Gladness	169				
O Sing a Song of Bethlehem	179				
Ye Who Claim the Faith of Jesus	197				
En el Frío Invernal	233				
Cold December Flies Away	233				
Hark! the Herald Angels Sing	240	101			
Love Came Down at Christmas	242				
We Sing of Your Glory				2011	
What a Mighty God We Serve				2021	
Great Is the Lord				2022	
The First Song of Isaiah				2030	
Thou Didst Leave Thy Throne				2100	
Psalm 148					
All Creatures of Our God and King	62	22			
How Great Thou Art	77	2	61		
O Lord My God! When I in Awesome Wonder	77	2	61		
Ye Watchers and Ye Holy Ones	90				
Praise the Lord Who Reigns Above	96		124		
God of the Sparrow God of the Whale	122	37	59		
Sing Praise to God Who Reigns Above	126		60		
Praise to the Lord, the Almighty	139	29	68		
I Sing the Almighty Power of God	152		65		

Scripture Hymn Title	UMH	MVPC	CLUW	TFWS	SOZ
I Love to Tell the Story	156	56			
Good Christian Friends, Rejoice	224		155		
Let All Things Now Living				2008	
Let Us with a Joyful Mind				2012	
Come, Rejoice in God				2017	
Praise the Lord with the Sound of Trumpet				2020	
What a Mighty God We Serve				2021	
Great Is the Lord				2022	
Halle, Halle, Halleluja				2026	
Clap Your Hands				2028	
Glory to God				2033	
Praise, Praise, Praise the Lord				2035	
Sing a New Song to the Lord				2045	
We Will Glorify the King of Kings				2087	
The Trees of the Field				2279	

Hebrews 2:10-18

Scripture Hymn Title	UMH	MVPC	CLUW	TFWS	SOZ
Thou Hidden Source of Calm Repose	153		346		
All Praise to Thee, for Thou, O King Divine	166				
Canticle of Christ's Obedience	167				
At the Name of Jesus Every Knee Shall Bow	168				
In Thee Is Gladness	169				
O Sing a Song of Bethlehem	179				
Jesús Es Mi Rey Soberano	180	54			
O Jesus, My King and My Sovereign	180	54			
Break Forth, O Beauteous Heavenly Light	223				
The Friendly Beasts	227				
Jesus, Our Brother, Strong and Good	227				
En El Frío Invernal	233				
Cold December Flies Away	233				
Rock-a-Bye, My Dear Little Boy	235				
That Boy-Child of Mary	241				
Once in Royal David's City	250		159		
O Love, How Deep, How Broad, How High	267				

Scripture Hymn Title	UMH	MVPC	CLUW	TFWS	SOZ
Lord, Who Throughout These Forty Days	269		181		
My Faith Looks Up to Thee	452				215
I Want Jesus to Walk with Me	521		104		95
Glory to God				2033	
Thou Didst Leave Thy Throne				2100	

Matthew 2:13-23

Scripture Hymn Title	UMH	MVPC	CLUW	TFWS	SOZ
Guide Me, O Thou Great Jehovah	127				
He Leadeth Me: O Blessed Thought	128	237			
O Sing a Song of Bethlehem	179				
What Child Is This	219	112	154		
Break Forth, O Beauteous Heavenly Light	223				
En el Frío Invernal	233				
Cold December Flies Away	233				
Rock-a-Bye, My Dear Little Boy	235				
Hark! the Herald Angels Sing	240	101			
Love Came Down at Christmas	242				
Joy to the World, the Lord Is Come!	246	100	161		
Once in Royal David's City	250		159		
Our Parent, by Whose Name	447				
We'll Understand It Better By and By	525	317			55
We Are Tossed and Driven on the Restless Sea of Time	525	317			55
God of Grace and God of Glory	577	287			
O Day of Peace that Dimly Shines	729				
Star-Child				2095	
Joseph Dearest, Joseph Mine				2099	
Thou Didst Leave Thy Throne				2100	

December 31, 2007 (Watch Night)

Scripture Hymn Title	UMH	MVPC	CLUW	TFWS	SOZ
Ecclesiastes 3:1-13					
For the Fruits of This Creation	97				
O God, Our Help in Ages Past	117				
Great Is Thy Faithfulness	140	30	81		
All Things Bright and Beautiful	147		63		
Forth in Thy Name, O Lord, I Go	438				
By Gracious Powers So Wonderfully Sheltered	517				
Beams of Heaven as I Go	524				10, 207
God of the Ages	698	377			
Hymn of Promise	707	338	392		
In the Bulb There Is a Flower	707	338	392		
From the Rising of the Sun				2024	
I Was There to Hear Your Borning Cry				2051	
For One Great Peace				2185	
In His Time				2203	
Psalm 8					
All Creatures of Our God and King	62	22			
Praise, My Soul, the King of Heaven	66				
O Lord My God! When I in Awesome Wonder	77	2	61		
How Great Thou Art	77	2	61		
Joyful, Joyful, We Adore Thee	89	5	75		
For the Beauty of the Earth	92	8			
For the Fruits of This Creation	97				
God, Whose Love Is Reigning o'er Us	100		73		
O God, Our Help in Ages Past	117				
O God in Heaven, Grant to Thy Children	119		227		

187

Scripture Hymn Title	UMH	MVPC	CLUW	TFWS	SOZ
Children of the Heavenly Father	141		335		
Many and Great, O God, Are Thy Things	148	50	71		
God Created Heaven and Earth	151				
I Sing the Almighty Power of God	152		65		
Creator of the Earth and Skies	450				
Prayer Is the Soul's Sincere Desire	492				
O God Beyond All Praising				2009	
Great Is the Lord				2022	
How Majestic Is Your Name				2023	
From the Rising of the Sun				2024	
Awesome God				2040	
Amen, We Praise Your Name, O God				2067	
Glory to God in the Highest				2276	

Revelation 21:1-6*a*

Scripture Hymn Title	UMH	MVPC	CLUW	TFWS	SOZ
O God, Our Help in Ages Past	117				
There's Something About That Name	171	74			
There's a Spirit in the Air	192				
O Let the Son of God Enfold You	347	190	91		
Spirit Song	347	190	91		
This Is a Day of New Beginnings	383	208	311		
Love Divine, All Loves Excelling	384				
O Come and Dwell in Me	388				
For the Healing of the Nations	428				
My Faith Looks Up to Thee	452				215
Come, Ye Disconsolate, Where'er Ye Languish	510				
Beams of Heaven as I Go	524				10, 207
We Shall Overcome	533		140		127
Here, O My Lord, I See Thee	623				
This Is the Feast of Victory	638				
Sing with All the Saints in Glory	702		382		
Soon and Very Soon	706		385		198
Come, Let Us Join Our Friends Above	709		387		
I Want to Be Ready	722				151
O Holy City, Seen of John	726		390		
O What their Joy and their Glory Must Be	727				
From the Rising of the Sun				2024	

Scripture Hymn Title	UMH	MVPC	CLUW	TFWS	SOZ
Awesome God				2040	
Open Our Eyes				2086	
We Will Glorify the King of Kings				2087	
All Who Hunger				2126	
You Who Are Thirsty				2132	
Blessed Quietness				2142	
O Freedom				2194	
Joy Comes with the Dawn				2210	
I'll Fly Away				2282	
For All the Saints				2283	
Joy in the Morning				2284	

Matthew 25:31-46

Scripture Hymn Title	UMH	MVPC	CLUW	TFWS	SOZ
How Can We Name a Love	111				
O God, Our Help in Ages Past	117				
We Gather Together to Ask the Lord's Blessing	131	361			
Christ Is the World's Light	188				
There's a Spirit in the Air	192				
Jesus' Hands Were Kind Hands	273		176		
Crown Him with Many Crowns	327	157			
Where Cross the Crowded Ways of Life	427	296			
For the Healing of the Nations	428				
Jesu, Jesu, Fill Us with Your Love	432	288	179		
All Who Love and Serve Your City	433				
Cuando El Pobre Nada Tiene	434	301	138		
When the Poor Ones Who Have Nothing	434	301	138		
Come, Ye Disconsolate, Where'er Ye Languish	510				
Forward Through the Ages	555				
Lord, Whose Love Through Humble Service	581				
Rescue the Perishing	591				
When the Church of Jesus Shuts Its Outer Door	592				
Come, Sinners, to the Gospel Feast (Communion)	616				
I Come With Joy to Meet My Lord	617				
Come, Ye Thankful People, Come	694		241		

Scripture Hymn Title	UMH	MVPC	CLUW	TFWS	SOZ
God Weeps				2048	
Shout to the Lord				2074	
Carol of the Epiphany				2094	
Star-Child				2095	
All Who Hunger				2126	
Sunday's Palms Are Wednesday's Ashes				2138	
What Does the Lord Require of You				2174	
Together We Serve				2175	
Wounded World that Cries for Healing				2177	
Here Am I				2178	
For One Great Peace				2185	
Now It Is Evening				2187	
People Need the Lord				2244	
In Remembrance of Me				2254	
As We Gather at Your Table				2268	
Come, Share the Lord				2269	

The United Methodist General Board of Discipleship, Center for Worship Resourcing; PO Box 340003; Nashville, TN 37203-0003
Toll-free Telephone 877-899-2780, ext. 7070; Email Address: WorshipCenter@gbod.org; Worship and Music Website http://www.umcworship.org

Sun	Mon	Tue	Wed	Thu	Fri	Sat
Call to Prayer and Self-Denial (any period during Jan-Mar)	**1** New Year's Day Eccl 3:1-13; Ps 8 (*UMH* 743); Rev 21:1-6a; Mt 25:31-46	**2**	**3**	**4**	**5**	**6** Epiphany Day (may observe on Dec 31, 2006) Isa 60:1-6; Ps 72:1-7, 10-14 (*UMH* 795); Eph 3:1-12; Mt 2:1-12
7 Baptism of the Lord; 1st Sun after Epiphany Isa 43:1-7; Ps 29 (*UMH* 761); Acts 8:14-17; Lk 3:15-17, 21-22	**8**	**9**	**10**	**11**	**12**	**13**
14 2nd Sun after Epiph Isa 62:1-5; Ps 36:5-10 (*UMH* 771); 1 Cor 12:1-11; Jn 2:1-11	**15** Martin Luther King, Jr Day	**16**	**17**	**18** Week of Prayer for Christian Unity, Jan 18-25	**19**	**20**
21 3rd Sun after Epiph Neh 8:1-3, 5-6, 8-10; Ps 19 (*UMH* 750); 1 Cor 12:12-31a; Lk 4:14-21	**22**	**23**	**24**	**25**	**26**	**27**
28 4th Sun after Epiph Jer 1:4-10; Ps 71:1-6 (*UMH* 794); 1 Cor 13:1-13; Lk 4:21-30	**29**	**30**	**31**			

Yearly dates to be determined by the annual conference:
- Christian Education Sunday
- Rural Life Sunday
- Disability Awareness Sunday
- International Day of Prayer for the Persecuted Church

February   2007

The United Methodist General Board of Discipleship, Center for Worship Resourcing; PO Box 340003; Nashville, TN 37203-0003
Toll-free Telephone 877-899-2780, ext. 7070; Email Address: WorshipCenter@gbod.org; Worship and Music Website http://www.umcworship.org

Sun	Mon	Tue	Wed	Thu	Fri	Sat
Feb: Black History Month	Brotherhood/Sisterhood Week: 3rd week of Feb			**1**	**2** Groundhog Day	**3**
4 5th Sun after Epiph Is 6:1-13; Ps 138 (UMH 853); 1 Cor 15:1-11; Lk 5:1-11	**5**	**6**	**7**	**8**	**9**	**10**
11 6th Sun after Epiph Jer 17:5-10; Ps 1 (UMH 738); 1 Cor 15:12-20; Lk 6:17-26	**12** Lincoln's Birthday	**13**	**14** Valentine's Day	**15**	**16**	**17**
18 Transfiguration Sun Ex 34:29-35; Ps 99 (UMH 819); 2 Cor 3:12-4:2; Lk 9:28-43	**19** Presidents Day	**20**	**21** Ash Wednesday Joel 2:1-2, 12-17 (or Is 58:1-12); Ps 51:1-17 (UMH 785); 2 Cor 5:20b-6:10; Mt 6:1-6, 16-21	**22** Washington's Birthday	**23**	**24**
25 1st Sun in Lent Deut 26:1-11; Ps 91:1-2, 9-16 (UMH 810); Rom 10:8b-13; Lk 4:1-13	**26**	**27**	**28**			

March

The United Methodist General Board of Discipleship, Center for Worship Resourcing; PO Box 340003, Nashville, TN 37203-0003
Toll-free Telephone 877-899-2780, ext. 7070; Email Address: WorshipCenter@gbod.org; Worship and Music Website http://www.umcworship.org

2007

Sun	Mon	Tue	Wed	Thu	Fri	Sat
Mar. Women's History Month				1	2 John Wesley d. 1791 World Day of Prayer	3
4 2nd Sunday in Lent Gen 15:1-12, 17-18; Ps 27 (*UMH 758*); Phil 3:17-4:1; Lk 13:31-35 (or Lk 9:28-36)	5	6	7	8	9	10
11 3rd Sun in Lent Girl Scout Sunday Is 55:1-9, Ps 63:1-8 (*UMH 788*); 1 Cor 10:1-13; Lk 13:1-9 Daylight Saving Time Begins	12	13	14	15	16	17 St. Patrick's Day
18 4th Sunday in Lent One Great Hour of Sharing Josh 5:9-12; Ps 32 (*UMH 766*); 2 Cor 5:16-21; Lk 15:1-3, 11b-32	19	20	21	22	23	24
25 5th Sunday in Lent Is 43:16-21; Ps 126 (*UMH 847*); Phil 3:4b-14; Jn 12:1-8	26	27	28	29 Charles Wesley d. 1788	30	31

April

The United Methodist General Board of Discipleship, Center for Worship Resourcing; PO Box 340003; Nashville, TN 37203-0003
Toll-free Telephone 877-899-2780, ext. 7070; Email Address: WorshipCenter@gbod.org; Worship and Music Website: http://www.umcworship.org

2007

Sun	Mon	Tue	Wed	Thu	Fri	Sat
1 Palm/Passion Sunday (see box below)	**2** Holy Monday Is 42:1-9, Ps 36:5-11; Heb 9:11-15; Jn 12:1-11	**3** Holy Tuesday Is 49:1-7; Ps 71:1-14; 1 Cor 1:18-31; Jn 12:20-36	**4** Holy Wednesday Is 50:4-9a; Ps 70; Heb 12:1-3; Jn 13:21-32	**5** Holy Thursday Ex 12:1-14; Ps 116:1-2, 12-19; 1 Cor 11:23-26; Jn 13:1-17, 31b-35	**6** Good Friday Is 52:13-53:12; Ps 22; Heb 10:16-25; Jn 18:1-19:42	**7** Holy Saturday Easter Vigil (see box below) Job 14:1-14; Ps 31:1-4, 15-16; 1 Pet 4:1-8; Mt 27:57-66
8 Easter Day Acts 10:34-43 (or Isa 65:17-25); Ps 118:1-2, 14-24 (UMH 839); 1 Cor 15:19-26; Jn 20:1-18 (or Lk 24:1-12)	**9**	**10**	**11**	**12**	**13**	**14**
15 2nd Sun of Easter Acts 5:27-32; Ps 150 (UMH 862); Rev 1:4-8; Jn 20:19-31	**16** USA Federal Income Tax Due	**17**	**18**	**19**	**20**	**21**
22 3rd Sun of Easter Native American Ministries Sunday; Earth Day, Festival of God's Creation; Acts 9:1-20; Ps 30 (UMH 762); Rev 5:11-14; Jn 21:1-19	**23**	**24**	**25** Administrative Assistants' Day	**26**	**27** Arbor Day	**28**
29 4th Sun of Easter Acts 9:36-43; Ps 23 (UMH 754); Rev 7:9-17; Jn 10:22-30	**30**	March: Women's History Month				

PALM/PASSION SUNDAY: Liturgy of the Palms: Lk 19:28-40; Ps 118:1-2, 19-29 (UMH 839) *Liturgy of the Passion:* Is 50:4-9a; Ps 31:9-16 (UMH 764); Phil 2:5-11; Lk 22:14-23:56 (or Lk 23:1-49)

EASTER VIGIL: The number of readings may vary, but Exodus 14 and at least two other readings from the Old Testament should be used in addition to the New Testament readings. *Old Testament Readings and Psalms:* Gen 1:1-2:4a; Is 55:1-11; Ps 136:1-9, 23-26 or Ps 33 (UMH 767); Is 12:2-6; Gen 7:1-5, 11-18; 8:6-18; 9:8-13; Ezek 36:24-28; Ps 46 (UMH 780); Ps 42 (UMH 777); Gen 22:1-18; Ezek 37:1-14; Ps 16 (UMH 748); Ps 143 (UMH 856); Ex 14:10-31; 15:20-21; Ex 15:1b-13, 17-18 (UMH 135); *Second Reading and Psalm:* Rom 6:3-11; Ps 114 (UMH 835); *Gospel Reading:* Lk 24:1-12

May 2007

The United Methodist General Board of Discipleship, Center for Worship Resourcing; PO Box 340003, Nashville, TN 37203-0003
Toll-free Telephone 877-899-2780, ext. 7070; Email Address: WorshipCenter@gbod.org; Worship and Music Website http://www.umcworship.org

Sun	Mon	Tue	Wed	Thu	Fri	Sat
May: Asian Pacific American Heritage Month; Christian Home Month	National Family Week, May 7-13	1	2	3 National Day of Prayer	4 May Fellowship Day	5
6 5th Sun of Easter Golden Cross Sunday Acts 11:1-18; Ps 148 (*UMH* 861); Rev 21:1-6; Jn 13:31-35	7	8	9	10	11	12
13 6th Sun of Easter Mothers' Day; Festival of the Christian Home; Acts 16:9-15; Ps 67 (*UMH* 791); Rev 21:10, 22–22:5; Jn 14:23-29 (or Jn 5:1-9)	14	15	16	17 Ascension Day (may be used May 20) Acts 1:1-11; Ps 47 (*UMH* 781) or Ps 110; Eph 1:15-23; Lk 24:44-	18	19 Armed Forced Day
20 7th Sun of Easter Heritage Sunday Acts 16:16-34; Ps 97 (*UMH* 816); Rev 22:12-14, 16-17, 20-21; Jn 17:20-26	21	22	23	24 Aldersgate Day	25	26
27 Pentecost Acts 2:1-21; Ps 104:24-34, 35b (*UMH* 826); Rom 8:14-17; Jn 14:8-17, (25-27)	28 Memorial Day	29	30	31		

The United Methodist General Board of Discipleship, Center for Worship Resourcing; PO Box 340003; Nashville, TN 37203-0003
Toll-free Telephone 877-899-2780, ext. 7070; Email Address: WorshipCenter@gbod.org; Worship and Music Website http://www.umcworship.org

Sun	Mon	Tue	Wed	Thu	Fri	Sat
					1	2
3 Trinity Sunday 1st Sun after Pent Peace with Justice Sun Prov 8:1-4, 22-31; Ps 8 (*UMH* 743); Rom 5:1-5; Jn 16:12-15	4	5	6	7	8	9
10 2nd Sun after Pent 1 Kgs 17:8-24; Ps 146 (*UMH* 858); Gal 1:11-24; Lk 7:11-17	11	12	13	14 Flag Day	15	16
17 3rd Sun after Pent Fathers' Day John Wesley b. 1703 1 Kgs 21:1-21*a*; Ps 5:1-8 (*UMH* 742); Gal 2:15-21; Lk 7:36-8:3	18	19	20	21	22	23
24 4th Sun after Pent 1 Kgs 19:1-15*a*; Ps 42 (*UMH* 777); Gal 3:23-29; Lk 8:26-39	25	26	27	28	29	30

July 2007

The United Methodist General Board of Discipleship, Center for Worship Resourcing; PO Box 340003; Nashville, TN 37203-0003
Toll-free Telephone 877-899-2780, ext. 7070; Email Address: WorshipCenter@gbod.org; Worship and Music Website http://www.umcworship.org

Sun	Mon	Tue	Wed	Thu	Fri	Sat
1 5th Sun after Pent 2 Kgs 2:1-2, 6-14; Ps 77:1-2, 11-20 (*UMH* 798), Gal 5:1, 13-25; Lk 9:51-62	**2**	**3**	**4** U.S.A. Independence Day	**5**	**6**	**7**
8 6th Sun after Pent 2 Kgs 5:1-14; Ps 30 (*UMH* 762); Gal 6:1-16; Lk 10:1-11, 16-20	**9**	**10**	**11**	**12**	**13**	**14**
15 7th Sun after Pent Amos 7:7-17; Ps 82 (*UMH* 804); Col 1:1-14; Lk 10:25-37	**16**	**17**	**18**	**19**	**20**	**21**
22 8th Sun after Pent Parents' Day Amos 8:1-12; Ps 52; Col 1:15-28; Lk 10:38-42	**23**	**24**	**25**	**26**	**27**	**28**
29 9th Sun after Pent Great Day of Singing Hosea 1:2-10; Ps 85 (*UMH* 806); Col 2:6-19; Lk 11:1-13	**30**	**31**				

August   2007

The United Methodist General Board of Discipleship, Center for Worship Resourcing; PO Box 340003; Nashville, TN 37203-0003
Toll-free Telephone 877-899-2780, ext. 7070; Email Address: WorshipCenter@gbod.org; Worship and Music Website http://www.umcworship.org

Sun	Mon	Tue	Wed	Thu	Fri	Sat
			1	2	3	4
5 10th Sun after Pent Hosea 11:1-11; Ps 107:1-9, 43; Col 3:1-11; Lk 12:13-21	6	7	8	9	10	11
12 11th Sun after Pent Is 1:1, 10-20; Ps 50:1-8, 22-23 (*UMH 783*); Heb 11:1-3, 8-16; Lk 12:32-40	13	14	15	16	17	18
19 12th Sun after Pent Is 5:1-7; Ps 80:1-2, 8-19 (*UMH 801*); Heb 11:29-12:2; Lk 12:49-56	20	21	22	23	24	25
26 13th Sun after Pent Jer 1:4-10; Ps 71:1-6 (*UMH 794*); Heb 12:18-29; Lk 13:10-17	27	28	29	30	31	

September

2007

The United Methodist General Board of Discipleship, Center for Worship Resourcing; PO Box 340003; Nashville, TN 37203-0003
Toll-free Telephone 877-899-2780, ext. 7070; Email Address: WorshipCenter@gbod.org; Worship and Music Website http://www.umcworship.org

Sun	Mon	Tue	Wed	Thu	Fri	Sat
Hispanic Heritage Month: Sep 15-Oct 15						1
2 14th Sun after Pent Jer 2:4-13; Ps 81:1, 10-16 (*UMH* 803); Heb 13:1-8, 15-16; Lk 14:1, 7-14	3 Labor Day	4	5	6	7	8
9 15th Sun after Pent Jer 18:1-11; Ps 139:1-6, 13-18 (*UMH* 854); Phil 1-21; Lk 14:25-33	10	11 Patriot Day	12	13	14	15
16 16th Sun after Pent Jer 4:11-12, 22-28; Ps 14 (*UMH* 746); 1 Tim 1:12-17; Lk 15:1-10	17	18	19	20	21	22
23 17th Sun after Pent Jer 8:18-9:1; Ps 79:1-9; 1 Tim 2:1-7; Lk 16:1-13	24	25	26	27	28	29
30 18th Sun after Pent Jer 32:1-3a, 6-15; Ps 91:1-6, 14-16 (*UMH* 810); 1 Tim 6:6-19; Lk 16:19-31						

October   2007

The United Methodist General Board of Discipleship, Center for Worship Resourcing; PO Box 340003; Nashville, TN 37203-0003
Toll-free Telephone 877-899-2780, ext. 7070; Email Address: WorshipCenter@gbod.org; Worship and Music Website http://www.umcworship.org

Sun	Mon	Tue	Wed	Thu	Fri	Sat
Hispanic Heritage Month: Sep 15 - Oct 15 Children's Sabbath: 2nd weekend in Oct	**1**	**2**	**3**	**4**	**5**	**6**
7 19th Sun after Pent World Communion Day; Lam 1:1-6; Ps 137 (*UMH 852*); 2 Tim 1:1-14; Lk 17:5-10	**8** Canada Thanksgiving Day; Columbus Day Deut 26:1-11; Ps 100 (*UMH 821*); Phil 4:4-9; Jn 6:25-35	**9**	**10**	**11**	**12** Children's Sabbath	**13** Children's Sabbath
14 20th Sun after Pent Children's Sabbath Jer 29:1, 4-7; Ps 66:1-12 (*UMH 790*); 2 Tim 2:8-15; Lk 17:11-19	**15**	**16**	**17**	**18**	**19**	**20**
21 21st Sun after Pent Laity Sunday Jer 31:27-34; Ps 119:97-104 (*UMH 840*); 2 Tim 3:14-4:5; Lk 18:1-8	**22**	**23**	**24** United Nations Day	**25**	**26**	**27**
28 22nd Sun after Pent Joel 2:23-32; Ps 65 (*UMH 789*); 2 Tim 4:6-8, 16-18; Lk 18:9-14	**29**	**30**	**31** Reformation Day; Halloween			

November 2007

The United Methodist General Board of Discipleship, Center for Worship Resourcing; PO Box 340003, Nashville, TN 37203-0003
Toll-free Telephone 877-899-2780, ext. 7070; Email Address: WorshipCenter@gbod.org; Worship and Music Website http://www.umcworship.org

Sun	Mon	Tue	Wed	Thu	Fri	Sat
Nov 11: International Day of Prayer for the Persecuted Church	Nov 11-18: National Bible Week			**1** All Saints Day (may be used Sun, Nov 4) Dan 7:1-3, 15-18; Ps 149 (or Ps 150, *UMH* 862); Eph 1:11-23; Lk 6:20-31	**2** World Community Day	**3**
4 23rd Sun after Pent Hab 1:1-4; 2:1-4; Ps 119:137-144 (*UMH* 840); 2 Thess 1:1-4, 11-12; Lk 19:1-10 Daylight Saving Time Ends	**5**	**6** Election Day	**7**	**8**	**9**	**10**
11 24th Sun after Pent Veterans Day; Organ & Tissue Donor Sunday Hag 1:15b-2:9; Ps 145:1-5, 17-21 (*UMH* 857); 2 Thess 2:1-5, 13-17; Lk 20:27-38	**12**	**13**	**14**	**15**	**16**	**17**
18 25th Sun after Pent Bible Sunday Is 65:17-25; Is 12 (or Ps 118, *UMH* 839); 2 Thess 3:6-13; Lk 21:5-19	**19**	**20**	**21**	**22** U.S.A. Thanksgiving Day Deut 26:1-11; Ps 100 (*UMH* 821); Phil 4:4-9; Jn 6:25-35	**23**	**24**
25 Christ the King/ Reign of Christ; UM Student Day Jer 23:1-6; Lk 1:68-79; Col 1:11-20; Lk 23:33-43	**26**	**27**	**28**	**29**	**30**	

December 2007

The United Methodist General Board of Discipleship, Center for Worship Resourcing; PO Box 340003, Nashville, TN 37203-0003
Toll-free Telephone 877-899-2780, ext. 7070; Email Address: WorshipCenter@gbod.org; Worship and Music Website http://www.umcworship.org

Sun	Mon	Tue	Wed	Thu	Fri	Sat
						1
2 1st Sun of Advent Is 2:1-5; Ps 122 (*UMH* 845); Rom 13:11-14; Mt 24:36-44	**3**	**4**	**5**	**6**	**7**	**8**
9 2nd Sun of Advent Is 11:1-10; Ps 72:1-7, 18-19 (*UMH* 795); Rom 15:4-13; Mat 3:1-12	**10**	**11**	**12**	**13**	**14**	**15**
16 3rd Sun of Advent Is 35:1-10; Ps 146:5-10 (*UMH* 858; or Lk 1:47-55); Jam 5:7-10; Mt 11:2-11	**17**	**18** Charles Wesley b. 1707	**19**	**20**	**21**	**22**
23 4th Sun of Advent Is 7:10-16; Ps 80:1-7, 17-19 (*UMH* 801); Rom 1:1-7; Mt 1:18-25	**24** Christmas Eve Is 9:2-7; Ps 96 (*UMH* 815); Tit 2:11-14; Lk 2:1-20	**25** Christmas Day Is 52:7-10; Ps 98 (*UMH* 818); Heb 1:1-12; Jn 1:1-14	**26**	**27**	**28**	**29**
30 1st Sun after Christmas Is 63:7-9; Ps 148 (*UMH* 861); Heb 2:10-18; Mt 2:13-23	**31** Watch Night Eccl 3:1-13; Ps 8 (*UMH* 743); Rev 21:1-6a; Mt 25:31-46					

2007